THE ILLUSTRATED MANUAL
OF SEX THERAPY

THE ILLUSTRATED MANUAL OF SEX THERAPY

Helen Singer Kaplan, M.D., Ph.D.

Drawings by David Passalacqua

A&W VISUAL LIBRARY

For information, address: Quadrangle/The New York
Times Book Co., 10 East 53rd Street, New York, N.Y. 10022.
Library of Congress Catalog Card Number: 75-45834
ISBN 0-89104-039-00
Drawings Copyright © 1975 David Passalacqua
Book design: Tere LoPrete
This edition published by arrangement with Quadrangle/
The New York Times Book Co.
Printed in the United States of America

To Aphrodite

Contents

List of Illustrations

Chapter 7 *Vaginismus*

Chapter 8 *Impotence—Erectile Dysfunction*

Chapter 9 *Retarded Ejaculation—Ejaculatory Overcontrol*

Chapter 10 *Premature Ejaculation— Inadequate Ejaculatory Control*

THE ILLUSTRATED MANUAL
OF SEX THERAPY

The Concept of Sex Therapy

The prescription of specific erotic experiences constitutes a distinctive feature of the new sex therapy. Various other forms of psychotherapy—notably analysis, marital therapy, and behavior therapy—have also been used to treat sexual dysfunctions. All of these rely exclusively on the therapeutic transactions which take place in the doctor's office. The analytic process produces an intense emotional interaction between the analyst and his analysand. The analysis of this relationship is used to foster insight into the unconscious conflicts and fears and desires which may lie at the root of the patient's sexual difficulty. The marriage therapist uses his observations of the interactions between the troubled couple as the basis of his inferences regarding the unconscious sources of a sexual problem. He confronts the couple with the destructive effects of their behavior on one another and also attempts to bring to their awareness the unconscious infantile and transferential forces which presumably have given rise to their neurotic behavior toward each other and also to the impairment of their sexual fulfillment. The behavior therapist does not deal with the concept of unconscious motivations. Rather he attempts to understand the behavioral conditions which have shaped and perpetuated a man's impotence or a woman's failure to reach orgasm. He tries to improve sexual functioning by changing the maladaptive reinforcement contingencies which have produced the sexually destructive anxieties and antierotic behavior patterns. Various techniques such as systematic desensitization to diminish anxiety, reinforcement of desirable erotic behavior, and adversive conditioning to eliminate patterns which are sexually destructive are used to implement this objective.

3

Sex therapy may employ all these various forms of psychotherapeutic interventions which are conducted in the doctor's office. However in sex therapy these are used in conjunction with prescribed sexual tasks which the couple practices in the privacy of their bedroom. It is the integrated use of systematically structured erotic experiences together with psychotherapeutic exploration of each partner's unconscious intrapsychic conflicts, as well as of the subtle dynamics of their interactions, which constitutes the unique feature and basic concept of sex therapy. In all probability the key to its effectiveness lies in this amalgam of experiential and dynamic modes.

The concepts and techniques of psychoanalysis, marital therapy, and behavior modification, which all have important places in the new sex therapy, are well documented and have been amply described in the literature. For these reasons these topics will not be covered in this volume. Indeed, practitioners of sex therapy should really be familiar with this material before they embark on the treatment of sexual dysfunctions.

Rather it is the objective of this book to describe the *erotic techniques* which are commonly employed in sex therapy, and also to offer some hypotheses regarding their rationale and the mechanisms of their action. In addition, the emotional impact of these exercises on patients, as well as the therapeutic implication of these emotional reactions, will be explored.

These tasks which are prescribed for sexually troubled couples, are not inhumane mechanical exercises. To the contrary, the erotic and sensuous interactions structured for the couple in sex therapy frequently evoke highly emotional responses from one or both partners. These responses are of profound significance for the psychotherapeutic process because they reveal crucial dynamics of the clinical problem which thus becomes immediately available for exploration during the psychotherapeutic sessions. For example, an impotent man cannot lie back, as he was instructed to do, and enjoy the tender caresses of his wife because he is made anxious by this experience and he becomes obsessed with ideas of rejection: "She is not enjoying this. . . . She will get tired. . . . She will think I am sick. . . . I must give her an orgasm. . . ." His fearful reactions to receiving pleasure from his wife and his defenses against this fear will become apparent both to his

4

therapist and to the couple themselves. Often engagement in such previously avoided experiences serves to confront the individual with the hidden insecurities which have been producing the failure of his erective reflexes at the very moment that he is so eager to function.

In this book I will describe some typical patient and spouse responses to each of the prescribed sexual tasks. In addition, I will explore some of the implications of these emotional reactions in terms of the causality of the sexual problems.

The couple's emotional responses to the prescribed sexual exercises represent a therapeutic challenge in that they constitute resistances and obstacles to therapy as well as a unique opportunity for effective therapeutic intervention. Therefore, I will also discuss some of the therapeutic strategies which may be used to deal with these emotional responses.

Finally the book contains illustrations of the techniques. In the past, both in training others to do this work and in prescribing sexual tasks to my patients, I have had to rely on my verbal descriptions. Often these do not convey the various positions with sufficient clarity and I have had to make sketches to illustrate what I was asking them to do. On some occasions members of the staff have actually had to demonstrate some of the more difficult positions during training seminars. It is the objective of the drawings contained in this book to provide clear illustrations of commonly suggested positions and erotic activities both for the didactic purposes of training and also for the instruction of patients. The drawings will, apart from merely illustrating specific positions, also, I hope, convey the beauty and humanity of sex, fundamentals to successful sex therapy.

The book, thus, is primarily an illustrated manual of the experiential aspects of sex therapy. In order to understand this material in a meaningful way, however, it is necessary to go into a little background regarding the nature of the sexual responses of men and women, the dynamics of sexual dysfunction, and some basic concepts of causality. These topics have been described in depth in my book, *The New Sex Therapy* (Quadrangle, 1974). These basics are summarized herein only for the purpose of setting the material on the tasks in its proper perspective.

I have also included a chapter on evaluation, i.e., the sexual examination and history. This is the structured interview by which one obtains the data which is necessary to formulate the problem. A sensitive multidimensional formulation is necessary to enable the therapist to make rational treatment decisions. Practiced in this manner, sex therapy is highly individualized and flexible. There should be no standardized treatment routine to be applied mechanically to all sexually dysfunctional couples. Each procedure, each task, each interpretation should have an explicit rational basis. Such an individualistic approach requires a rather special assessment technique, one which is focused on evaluating a couple's sexual *experience* rather than relying exclusively on obtaining descriptive mental status type of data.

Sex therapy, effective as it is for appropriate cases, is not indicated for all sexual difficulties. Some persons' sexual problems are too deeply rooted and some relationships are too hostile to be amenable to brief intervention. It is useful for the therapist to be aware of the limitations as well as of the strengths of this approach. Therefore some of the prognostic factors which seem to influence the outcome of sex therapy are also discussed in this book.

One of the serious limitations of sex therapy is that, with the exception of totally anorgastic females, treatment entails the participation of two cooperative individuals. As described in this book, the prescribed exercises which are a crucial ingredient of sex therapy are essentially structured interactions between sexual partners. They simply cannot be conducted alone. This poses a problem for the single person with a sexual dysfunction.

Some clinics have attempted to deal with this dilemma by providing surrogate partners—e.g., strangers who for a fee partake in the sexual exercises with the patient. There are advantages and disadvantages to this approach. The chief advantage is that it provides an opportunity for some inadequately functioning single persons to attain self-confidence and security in sexual functioning which will then enable them to seek a relationship. However, one of the prime objectives of sex therapy is to humanize the sexual relationship. Sex with a paid stranger, no matter how perfect it is mechanically, will not accomplish this. A preferable approach perhaps is by means of psychotherapy, to bring the person to that level of self-esteem where he will be free to

6

engage in a relationship with a woman even if he does not function perfectly. In my own clinical practice, when a dysfunctional patient who has no partner seeks help I do an evaluation and share my formulation with the patient. I also describe and explain the treatment which might be helpful in his case. Sometimes psychotherapy is offered as a reasonable alternative to sex therapy for the single patient, but sometimes it is not likely to be effective, at least in terms of the sexual symptom. The patient is of course not cured by this kind of consultation and counseling, but he is given a rational understanding of his problem and also the hope of resolution when and if he can form a suitable relationship.

In any work on sex therapy a word should be said about its narrow objective of improving sexual functioning. We should not feel apologetic for this because a person's erotic well-being is an extremely important aspect of human experience. Admittedly, however, it is only a limited aspect, and sex therapy should take cognizance of larger human issues. While we focus on sex, we should also be responsive to the wider psychic matrix of which sexuality is an integral and beautiful part.

I
BASIC ISSUES

I

The Nature and Causes of the Sexual Dysfunctions

The sexual responses in men and women transform the quiescent genitals into effective reproductive equipment. "The flaccid urinary penis is transformed into the erect reproductive phallus, while the dry potential vaginal space becomes an open, lubricated, and engorged recepticle."* On first inspection the sexual response of men and women appears to be a single event. In the male, erection proceeds to ejaculation. In the female, lubrication and swelling of the genitals culminates in orgasm. However, evidence suggests that the sexual response of both genders actually consists of two separate phases. These are analogous both anatomically and physiologically in both genders. They may be inhibited separately to produce different dysfunctional syndromes.

The first part of the sexual response consists of genital vasocongestion. The second, orgasm, is essentially a series of involuntary clonic contractions of the genital musculature.

In the male, erection is produced by a vasocongestion of penile blood vessels. Penile capillaries expand and special veinous channels close. Blood is trapped in special caverns of the penis, and this essentially hydraulic mechanism extends that organ. This response is mediated by the autonomic nervous system: arteriolar dilation is parasympathetically mediated, while closure of the veinous valves is probably controlled by sympathetic nerves. Orgasm is a separate response. In the male it comprises two components: emission and ejaculation.

* *The New Sex Therapy.* Helen S. Kaplan. Quadrangle, 1974.

11

Emission (which is perceived by men as the sensation of ejaculatory inevitability) consists of the reflex contraction of the internal reproductive organs. Contractions of the vasa deferentia, prostate, and seminal vesicles squeezes ejaculate into the posterior urethra. Emission is a sympathetically mediated response. A split second later ejaculation occurs. This consists of o.8-second contractions of the striated muscles at the base of the penis: the bulbo and ischio cavernosi muscles.

Two analogous events occur in women. In response to sexual arousal there is a vasocongestion of the blood vessels of the labia and tissues surrounding the vagina. This swelling is more diffuse than in the male. Females do not have special caverns, and instead of erection, female genital congestion produces the "orgasmic platform," localized perivaginal swelling. Genital vasocongestion is also responsible for vaginal lubrication which is actually a transudate of the fluid that accumulates in the pelvis during this arousal phase in females. In addition the smooth muscles of the internal vagina expand, causing an internal ballooning and extension of the vagina and a rise of the uterus. In contrast to the male, the female orgasm only has one component. Women lack the emission phase. However, the clonic phase is strictly analogous and consists of the o.8-second contractions of the ischio and bulbo cavernosi muscles as well as of the pubococcygeal muscles. Peripheral innervation of the female sexual response has not yet been studied, but it may be speculated by analogy that the female sexual responses are also governed by the autonomic nervous system.

When these responses or any of their component phases are impaired, sexual dysfunction results. There are six dysfunctions: three of the male and three of the female.

When the erectile response is impaired the man is *impotent*. The inhibition in impotence is confined to the erectile, vasocongestive component of the sexual response. The ability to ejaculate may be retained in impotence. There are also two ejaculatory disorders: *premature ejaculation* and *retarded ejaculation*. The premature ejaculator fails to acquire adequate voluntary control over his orgastic reflex. As as result he climaxes very rapidly. In contrast the patient with retarded ejaculation suffers from involuntary overcontrol. He has difficulty in releasing his ejaculatory reflex even though he receives adequate stimulation.

Vaginismus is a uniquely female complaint which has no analogy in the male. In this disorder the muscles guarding the vaginal entrance have been conditioned to respond spasmodically when any attempt at penetration is made. This condition makes intercourse impossible.

The other two female dysfunctions are analogous to impotence, on the one hand, and retarded ejaculation on the other. The *generally unresponsive* woman, like the man with erectile difficulty fails to respond to sexual stimulation with lubrication and genital vasocongestion. The woman who suffers from *orgastic dysfunction* like the man with retarded ejaculation experiences various degrees of difficulty in releasing her orgastic reflex, but is otherwise sexually responsive.

A Psychosomatic Concept of Sexual Dysfunction

The sexual responses are delicate and can easily be disrupted by negative affect or by psychological conflict and inhibition.

When a man is frightened or angry or tense at the moment that he is making love, his erectile or ejaculatory reflexes are likely to be impaired. For proper sexual functioning to occur a person must not only be free of intense negative affect, but must also be free of excessive cognitive control. In other words good sex requires a calm emotional state and *abandonment* to the erotic experience. This is also true of all other biological functions which are controlled by the autonomic nervous system. Digestion, respiration, and cardiovascular functions are similarly innervated by the visceral nerves and are similarly subject to impairment by emotional and cognitive factors. In other words these functional systems are also subject to psychosomatic disorders.

In the past it was believed that only profound neurotic conflict was capable of impairing the sexual responses. Severely pathogenic and regressive conflicts centering on unconscious, delusional, and infantile fears of injury if one were to enjoy sex were believed to be the sole vectors of sexual dysfunction. These conflicts were believed to originate in the patient's childhood before the age of five. Pathological interactions with parents which resulted in morbid fears and insecurities and the defenses erected against these were believed to hold the

13

key to all sexual difficulty. Not surprisingly, analytic treatment was designed to clarify these issues and bring them into the patient's conscious awareness in hope of resolving them. Only the resolution of deep unconscious conflict was believed to be capable of curing the sexual symptom.

Masters and Johnson and the behaviorists taught us that the roots of psychopathology often originate in far simpler ground. Performance anxiety, superficial insecurities, tensions due to poor communications with one's mate, anxiety born of misconceptions about the human sexual response also can and do cause a large proportion of the sexual difficulties we see in clinical practice. And this is eminently logical. For physiologically speaking, sexually disruptive anxiety is identical whether caused by return of oedipal taboos and fears of castration, or whether a man panics because he is afraid that a bout of alcohol-induced erectile difficulty will be repeated.

Actually, causality lies on a continuum which reaches from superficial anticipation of failure to the profound psychopathology which causes the sexual response to acquire dangerous symbolic meaning on an unconscious level. Concomitantly, effective intervention also can be described as falling on a continuum: from sex education and counseling, to sex therapy, to extensive reconstructive psychoanalytic treatment.

Our sexually repressed society, has until recently, failed to regard sex as a natural function. Thus accurate information about the sexual response has not been freely or widely available. This curtain of ignorance plus the highly emotional attitudes about erotic matters provide a fertile culture medium for the growth of ignorance, myths, and misconceptions. Myths are prevalent about ever-ready male functioning, vaginal orgasms, mutual climax, masturbation, fantasy, frigid women, and so on. A great deal of anxiety and guilt can be generated when there is a discrepancy between real experience and unrealistic expectation. Such misconceptions along with the emotional reactions which accompany them can produce sexual maladjustments and dysfunctions.

In addition, anxiety and guilt may cause a person to avoid sex and/or to restrict his or her sexual behavior. This deprives him of the opportunity of exploring and learning sexual techniques and attitudes which will please him and his partner.

Persons who suffer from ignorance about sexual techniques and malignant misconceptions can often be helped with simple sex education and counseling. This treatment mode entails dispelling misinformation and guilt and giving instruction in effective sexual techniques.

The causes of another group of dysfunctional patients run somewhat deeper. The sexual responses of this group are impaired by the fear of sexual *failure,* by a tendency to remain under *conscious control* during the sex act, by haunting fears of *rejection* should they fail to please the partner or to *"perform"* adequately. Yet they are free of deeper guilts and fears and marital hostilities. This group of patients are highly amenable to brief sex therapy which aims to create a secure, open, and comfortable sexual ambiance. The course of treatment in such cases tends to be uncomplicated. Interpretations are mainly supportive, aim at opening the couple's routes of communications, and are not often profoundly analytical. Results of sex therapy with this group of patients is excellent. Fortunately these constitute a sizable proportion of the patient population.

The next group of patients are more difficult to treat. They, too, suffer from fears of rejection and from performance anxiety. But in this group these fears are related to deeper insecurities. The sexual problem is associated with profound conflicts. Sex therapy must contend with fundamentally disturbed relationships between the genders. In this group of patients the self-esteem is more fragile; guilt arising from sex and pleasure is more tenacious.

These more difficult patients are still amenable to sex therapy, but only if the sex therapist is prepared to contend with disturbance on a deeper dynamic level. The therapist must be cognizant of the psychodynamics of unconscious conflicts and of the relationship of such conflicts to sexual difficulty. He must be skilled at working on the level of unconscious motivation. He must have the clinical judgment to decide: when to *bypass* such conflicts by providing the patient with defenses against anxiety and thereby sever the connection between deeper conflict and sexual functioning; when to attempt to *resolve* such conflict by active

15

interpretation and confrontation; when to *shift the emphasis* of treatment away from the experiential symptom-focused sex therapy into *psycho*therapy designed to resolve intrapsychic and marital dynamics while the therapist postpones actual sex therapy.

Finally there are some patients suffering from sexual dysfunctions which are not amenable to brief active intervention. Fortunately these seem to be relatively rare. The sexual problems of this group are tenaciously connected to profound marital and individual psychopathology. Their depressions are so deep, their paranoia so pervasive, their marital hostilities so malignant and antisexual, and their defenses so rigid and successful that they first need more extensive psychotherapeutic intervention, either analytic which aims to change basic emotional attitudes or marital: the goal of which is to resolve profound dyadic (couple) conflicts, before they can benefit from sex therapy.

2

The Sexual Evaluation

Assessment in medicine employs two main tools: history and examination. In diagnosing a patient's sexual problem we also rely on history and examination. However, the examination in sex therapy does not primarily employ physical inspection, palpation, and auscultation. Of course in some instances when it is indicated, physical examination of the sexual organs needs to be done, and the diagnosis may in some cases also depend on input from laboratory examinations. However in our sexual examination in contrast to examinations for other ailments, we rely most heavily on a sensitive and empathic assessment of the couple's *sexual experience,* as it is communicated to us by them in the consultation room. It is in this manner that we capture the signs, symptoms, and antecedents of the sexual dysfunction and obtain the data we need to assess the determinants of the person's problem. Perhaps some time in the future sex therapists will observe their patients in the act of lovemaking or inspect video tapes of their sexual activities. Until such a time the interview which is designed to assess the couple's sexual experience in detail and depth is an exquisitely sensitive and highly effective diagnostic tool.

After I obtain a couple's names, ages, address, and marital and family status I ask for the nature of the chief complaint and events of the onset of the problem. Then I evaluate their sexual experience.

Please tell me exactly what happens when you two make love. [They are often embarrassed and evasive.] I am sorry if this is embarrassing, but I can't really help you until I know exactly what is going on.

I pursue gently but firmly. My own attitude of sexual openness is transmitted and eases the inquiry. I encourage and reinforce openness, frank participation. Sometimes one partner is more able to communicate than the other. I note this for later reference, but for the sake of my inquiry I encourage the communicative one to begin. I continue until, in my mind's eye, I have a crystal clear and detailed picture of the physical acts which transpire between the couple. I persevere in order to also understand the emotional reactions of the partners, their fantasies, and the interplay between them.

If there are obscure areas I will persist and question until these are cleared up.

Yes, but *when* do you initiate actual intercourse? When *you* feel a certain level of excitement? When you think *he* is getting impatient? Both?

The process is very much like auscultating and percussing again and again until one has a clear mental picture of the inner anatomy and pathology of that coughing patient's chest.

Usually there has been a change in sexual responsiveness. Then I will conduct a similar assessment of both partners' prior sexual experiences.

What was it like before you had intercourse? When you were only necking? Before you had orgasm? Was it different with other women? With a prostitute? How are your masturbatory experiences different from when you are with your husband? Tell me what you experience when you masturbate.

When I have a clear image of the couple's sexual experience, as it exists now and as it evolved, I can begin to formulate their problem in my mind. This is a tentative formulation, but one which guides my questions toward particular pathways. For clinical purposes (as opposed to investigative objectives), the psychosexual history is most effective if it does not consist of a routine set of questions, but instead is problem oriented.

18

Medical and Psychiatric Evaluation

In the course of the sexual evaluation I always conduct a brief psychiatric examination as well as a medical history and drug survey. This is an essential part of the total evaluation, because medical and psychiatric problems such as diabetes or depression can be the major determinants of a sexual dysfunction.

MEDICAL SURVEY

One cannot assume that a sexual problem is psychogenic unless a possible physical etiology is ruled out. Some dysfunctions are seldom associated with organic factors. These include situational orgastic dysfunction and primary prematurity. But it has been estimated that low libido and impotence in 10 to 25 percent of cases are caused, at least in part, by medical and pharmacologic factors.

Any generally debilitating and/or painful *illness* will affect sexual functioning adversely. In addition endocrine disturbances which interfere with testosterone production or utilization also impair libido in both genders, and erection in the male. Therefore during my medical history I will always specifically question about the signs and symptoms of hepatic disease, pituitary and gonadal difficulties, and the like. Any illness which impairs blood supply to the pelvis and any interference with the pudendal or autonomic pelvic nerves interfere with sexual functioning. For this reason review of systems must be done to rule out circulatory disturbances, neurological illness, or surgical procedures which interfere with genital nerves and blood vessels, for example, perineal prostatectomy and sympathetetomies. Diabetes even in its early stages is the most common physical cause of erectile difficulties. For this reason a 2-h. glucose tolerance test is always ordered in all cases of impotence. In addition I always order a serum testosterone level and sometimes an estrogen and progesterone level as well in order to determine whether treatment with androgens as part of the sex therapy is indicated. Often a thyroid function test is also ordered.

Drugs and medicines are common unsuspected culprits in the sexual

19

dysfunctions. Four categories of medication are capable of impairing the sexual responses: antiandrogens, antiautonomic drugs (anticholinergics and antiadrenergics), narcotics, and excessive use of sedatives and alcohol.

These drugs act by a variety of mechanisms. Narcotics are general sedatives and also seem to exert a specific depressive effect on the sex areas of the brain. Alcohol is a general central nervous system depressant which like sedatives in general impairs sexuality along with other functions. When chronically ingested in high doses, it also causes neurologic damage which may be sexually destructive. The female hormones estrogen and progesterone, cyproterone, and the antihypertensive agents aldectazine and aldectone are antiandrogens which produce a chemical castration. These may lower libido in both genders and cause erection problems in males. Aldomet and other hypotensive agents paralyze the adrenergic nerves which mediate ejaculation and one aspect of erection and cause impotence in a large percentage of the patients who ingest them. The drugs used in the treatment of hypertension are particularly apt to contribute to sexual dysfunctions.

It is clear therefore that a sexual evaluation should include a survey of all medication taken by the patient. It is not wise to commence sex therapy if a patient is on medication which impairs the sexual response. Often medication can be changed to drugs which act effectively on the medical target symptom without producing sexually destructive side effects.

PSYCHIATRIC EXAMINATION

A brief psychiatric examination is conducted on *both* partners as part of the initial evaluation. This examination should yield three types of information: (1) The presence and nature of any psychopathology in either partner must be determined, (2) the quality of their relationship must be assessed, and (3) the therapist should emerge from the initial evaluation with a good idea of the precise role that the sexual symptom plays in the intrapsychic dynamics of each partner and in their marital interactions. These three factors must be understood before intervention can be conducted on a safe and rational basis.

Psychopathology

Many persons who seek help for their sexual dysfunctions are free of significant psychopathology. And their mates are also basically healthy emotionally. Prognosis with sex therapy is generally excellent with emotionally healthy couples, and the therapist can expect a fairly uncomplicated and rapid course of treatment.

But of course neurotic and psychotic persons also suffer from sexual dysfunctions, and the mates of dysfunctional persons may be emotionally disturbed. Psychopathology in either partner exerts strong influences on sexual functioning and on sex therapy: emotional difficulties affect the outcome, complicate treatment, and sometimes even preclude sex therapy altogether.

Sex therapy is contraindicated when *either* partner is in an active stage of a major psychiatric disorder. Clearly, florid schizophrenic reactions, blatant paranoia, and significant depression in *either* partner make sex therapy unfeasible. In fact injudicious intervention with a marginally compensated person may even precipitate a serious adverse reaction.

Sex therapy with persons who harbor major psychiatric disorders but *are well compensated* is not contraindicated providing the therapist is sensitive to and careful not to tamper with crucial defenses against the emergence of open illness. In fact, improved sexual functioning and a better marital relationship may result from successful sex therapy in such cases.

Neurotics and persons with personality disorders frequently are afflicted with symptoms of sexual dysfunction, and this group will make up a large bulk of patients in sex therapy clinics.

While, in general, neurotics with neurotic partners have a more guarded prognosis with sex therapy, many such couples can benefit from sex therapy in terms of improved sexual functioning. In evaluating such patients, in addition to assessing the specific sexual problem it is important for the therapist to formulate a picture of the deeper structure of the unconscious dynamics of both partners. He needs a clear concept of his patient's personality structure and his unconscious conflicts and defenses to guide his therapeutic intervention during sex therapy. He especially needs to know how to avoid mobilizing neurotic defenses and resistances. An astute assessment of which of his patient's conflicts must be resolved, and which ones can be bypassed, in order to liberate sexual functioning is very important in dealing with the neurotic segment of the patient population.

The Relationship Between Sexual Symptoms and Neurotic Conflicts

Effective sex therapy requires an understanding of the precise relationship *between the patient's unconscious neurotic conflicts and his sexual symptom.* In the past it had been assumed that all sexual symptoms were direct products of deep conflicts and that these conflicts had to be resolved before sexual functioning could improve. Our experience with sex therapy has shown that this concept is erroneous for practical purposes. The relationship between sexual symptoms and neurotic conflict is highly variable and complex. While it is, of course, true that some sexual dysfunction is a direct expression of neurotic conflict, this is certainly not universal. Sexual dysfunction often results from more superficial sources of anxiety—such as anticipation of failure to perform. This may occur in persons who also suffer from deeper problems. However, often there is *no direct* connection between the presenting sexual complaint, which may be caused by simple performance anxiety, and the patient's deeper neurotic problems. In such cases the prognosis with sex therapy is excellent. However, the sexual functioning and symptoms can in neurotic individuals acquire symbolic meaning or become utilized as a psychologic defense. When such is the case, the therapist can expect a difficult and stormy course of treatment. For example if a man's premature ejaculation unconsciously expresses his rebellion against his "wife-mother"; if a woman's failure to respond to her husband is a symbol of her yearning for a "superdaddy" whose love will repair her self-esteem, and so on; then the brief active intervention of sex therapy may meet tenacious obstacles and resistances. Fortunately sexual symptoms do not always serve as psychological defenses. Even those cases are not hopeless, however, because therapeutic techniques exist whereby such connections between unconscious conflict and sexual symptoms can sometimes be bypassed. In such cases the

22

benefits of sex therapy are limited to improvement of sexual functioning while the patient retains his basic neurosis. Finally the confrontation with deep sexual conflict which occurs in the process of sex therapy frequently opens the way for reconstructive psychotherapeutic resolution of the patient's basic problems.

The Relationship Between the Couple

The quality of the relationship between the couple who seek help for sexual problems is an important prognostic factor in the outcome of sex therapy. The therapist needs to understand the nature of the bond between them on both a superficial and a deeper level. A true love bond even in the presence of superficial bickering and petty differences improves the prognosis for sex therapy immensely, regardless of the specific clinical problem. Couples who love each other deeply really wish to function, to experience each other fully on a conscious as well as an unconscious level. For such loving couples sexual improvement poses no threat and creates no conflict. On the contrary the opposite is true if the relationship is essentially hostile, even if on the surface the interactions appear tranquil. In such cases the expressed wish for good sexual functioning runs counter to the unconscious need to hurt and to keep the mate at a distance. Such unconscious fears and angers will mobilize serious resistances and obstacles to therapy. How *can* a woman lovingly caress and pleasure a man at whom she is deeply angry? How could a man possibly be patient and gentle with a woman and allow himself to become aroused by her when he is fearful of intimacy and involvement with her? The depth and seriousness of such negative feelings and transactions must be assessed and dealt with in therapy. Sometimes they are insurmountable and preclude sex therapy, which after all requires the unambivalent cooperation of both partners. In other cases when negative feelings are based on resolvable fears and resentments, the therapist can deal with negative interactions successfully. In fact sex therapy provides a splendid opportunity to help a couple resolve marital difficulties when they are so motivated.

Apart from the quality of the couple's bond, a sexual dysfunction may play an important role in their marital system. Impotence may be a means of controlling the wife, and for her it may mean security in the relationship. When sexual dysfunction provides secondary gains in terms of stabilizing the marital system, one may expect intense emotional reactions and obstacles to treatment from either partner or from both.

THE PSYCHOSEXUAL EXAMINATION

The sexual inquiry is designed to give the therapist a detailed mental picture of the superficial as well as the deeper structure of the couple's sexuality. What "turns each on"? What "turns each off"? What are the fantasies and the unconscious hopes and fears of each?

Each partner is questioned in great detail about his sexual development. "Did his sexuality develop normally? When and how did he first experience erotic feelings? Was childhood sexuality suppressed? Was it associated with negative contingencies? At what age did masturbation commence? What were the early fantasies? What were his feelings about this? Any early overt sexual experiences? What was the family attitude toward masturbation? Toward sex? What was the first sexual experience like? Was it exciting? Guilt provoking? Did she "turn it off" or "go with it"? How did he function? What sorts of erotic situations have excited him in the past? When and under what circumstances has he failed to function? Or functioned well? How does *he* experience orgasm? How does *she*? How does she feel about clitoral stimulation? What vaginal sensations does she have on coitus? How does she feel about oral sex? About receiving stimulation? About giving stimulation? How about semen in her mouth? About her genital odors? What excites her most? What sorts of fears does she have? How does she feel about her body? breasts? How does she think he feels about her body? Does she think she takes too long to climax? Can he hold out long enough? Does he get an erection by touching her body? Does he need physical stimulation of his penis? How does she feel if he doesn't get an erection? How does he feel when she doesn't climax?"

It is the main purpose of this evaluation to provide a conceptual blueprint for therapeutic action. It is the strategy of sex therapy to modify the couple's sexual transactions so as to eliminate fear, guilt, and anxiety, and to maximize excitement and gratification. These are highly variable and individualistic matters. Only if the therapist has a clear image of the specific sources of stress which had impaired the free expression of the couple's sexuality can he intervene in a rational and individualistic manner.

The initial sexual evaluation no matter how skillfully done yields only a first approximation, a tentative hypothesis of the structure and dynamics of the couple's sexual difficulty. This view is refined, clarified, and corrected as therapy proceeds. The couple's reactions to the assigned sexual tasks illuminate hidden features of the couple's sexuality which are seldom totally revealed on the initial evaluation. I consider an initial evaluation successful if I feel secure in what I am doing in devising and prescribing the first structured interaction. If the issues are not sufficiently clarified by my verbal inquiry, I will often use a behavioral sig* as a *probe*. How do they respond to a sensate focus sig? With anxiety, pleasure, or eroticism? Much is learned from such responses and also from the couple's association to the structured interactions. The deeper and more subtle issues of a case usually do not become completely resolved in my mind until I have had the opportunity to observe the couple's experiences with some of the assigned tasks.

* Sig means "signa," the symbol used on pharmacists' prescription to note the directions to the patient about the use of medication.

II

THE SEXUAL
EXERCISES

A. An Erotic Technique Used for Many Dysfunctions

3

Sensate Focus I – Pleasuring

The term "sensate focus," invented by Masters and Johnson, is a rather clumsy term for a simple and beautiful activity. It means that the couple desists from intercourse and orgasm for several days or weeks during which time they gently caress each other's bodies and genitals. I prefer the term "pleasuring" (which was also introduced into the literature by Masters and Johnson). Many authorities believe that these exercises are among their most significant clinical innovations.

Application of Sensate Focus—Pleasuring

Masters and Johnson state in their book, *Human Sexual Inadequacy* (Little, Brown, and Co., 1970), that all the couples they treated, regardless of the nature of their complaint or of the psychodynamics of their problem, start the experiential aspect of their treatment regimen with the sensate focus exercises. This is usually prescribed on day three of the therapeutic procedure, after the nature of the sexual problem has been discussed with the couple by the cotherapists during the "round-table" meeting. I have also been impressed with the profound therapeutic impact the sensate focus experience has on many persons, and I use it extensively in sex therapy. However, I do so in a more flexible and individualistic manner. I prescribe pleasuring only when it seems specifically indicated by the nature of the dysfunction and by the requirements of the dynamics of that particular case. Thus for example I do not routinely prescribe pleasuring at all for couples whose chief complaint is vaginismus or premature ejaculation or for totally inorgasmic women.

For these dysfunctions I employ the specific indicated therapeutic tasks which will be described later: dilatation, Semans' maneuver, and self-stimulation respectively. However I may of course also prescribe pleasuring in such cases but only if it is really needed. The timing of the prescription is also flexible and dictated by dynamic considerations. Therefore, I may not use pleasuring as the initial experience, but only after the case has progressed. Thus for example I might prescribe sensate focus for a couple after the man has already attained a good degree of ejaculatory control by means of the Semans' exercises, or if the couple continues to avoid tactile contact, or if they are too orgasm-oriented, or if they need to be confronted with their anxiety about intimacy, and so on. For other dysfunctions sensate focus is employed more often.

I commonly prescribe pleasuring in the initial stages of the treatment of erectile disorders, general nonresponsivity of women, and relative orgastic inhibitions. But I do not do this routinely because often other types of experiences seem to be more rational. For example in treating some particularly defended impotent patients, I might avoid gentle, slow stimulation because in some men this causes excessive anxiety. I might use other forms of stimulation such as erotic films or art literature to promote arousal in such cases.

Rationale

The mechanism of action of sensate focus is not completely clear. Probably there are various dynamics to account for the profound effects which these seemingly simple and gentle exercises frequently evoke. These effects may be understood on several conceptual levels.

Pleasuring—Woman face up

The pleasuring prescription often (though by no means always) produces a reduction of tension in the sexual transactions. Each partner is freed of the expectation that he/she must produce an adequate response in himself and in his partner. He doesn't *need* to have an erection, it is *not her duty* to *make* him have one. Neither is *allowed,* much less pressured, to reach orgasm. Failure is practically impossible under these circumstances. Furthermore medical authority has given permission, indeed *prescribed* pleasure. From the perspective of learning theory this creates conditions ideal for the *extinction* of sexual anxiety. Under such relaxed, easy conditions old fears can be extinguished. Anticipatory anxiety related to failure and injury can gradually be reduced. Under these circumstances the emergent pleasurable responses also reinforce more adequate sexual behavior.

Apart from their teaching function, the sensate focus exercises are also intrinsically enjoyable and provide the couple with the opportunity to give and receive pleasure from each other. Gentle stroking and nuzzling and caressing seem to evoke highly pleasurable emotional responses from most persons, providing there is no significant conflict about the pleasuring experience. This is true on the infrahuman as well as on the human level. Petting a dog is highly rewarding and may be used as reinforcement, and "gentling" young laboratory animals is a well-known technique for producing tame and cooperative experimental subjects. Clinical evidence suggests that mutual, gentle, tactile stimulation can enhance the affectionate *bond* between people. Again on an infrahuman level, Harlow found tactile contact to be an important component in the affectionate bonds developed by baby chimps. One tends to respond with love to a person who gently caresses and pleasures one. Tender, tactile contact seems to increase intimacy and mutual involvement. Stringent experimentation is of course needed to support these clinical impressions.

Thus sensate focus is a learning experience whereby pleasurable responses are reinforced and sexual anxiety is diminished because the fear of failure is removed. An additional feature apart from the intrinsic value of this experience relates to psychodynamics of the couple's psychosexual problems. In gently caressing each other the couple may be confronted with an experience which they have previously avoided because physical intimacy arouses anxiety in one or both partners. With the arousal of such anxiety and of the defenses this anxiety elicits, both become subject to psychotherapeutic exploration, and this is very important for the therapy of all but the most simple cases of sexual dysfunction.

It is the clarification of such negative emotional responses which is the crux of intervention in the therapy of most cases of sexual dysfunction. This point will be elaborated in a later section of this chapter which deals with some typical patient responses to sensate focus.

Directions

If a therapist is open and essentially conflict free about sex and pleasure, he is likely to give the pleasuring directions in an effective manner. Conversely, patients are likely to respond negatively to a therapist's lack of ease or to his own anxiety.

Here is the usual way I give these directions. They vary of course with the couple, their level of anxiety, the nature of psychopathology, if any, and their socioeconomic and cultural backgrounds. My method should not be imitated unless it seems natural. Each therapist should develop his own individual style of communication.

"First, I do not want you to have intercourse or orgasm for a little while. How do you feel about that?" (The therapist should then deal with any feelings expressed.) "You *will* have physical contact however, of a very special kind. After dinner tonight, when all your responsibilities are done, I want you both to take showers and then go to bed without any clothes on. Then I want you to caress each other. First you caress her." (The choice of who does the pleasuring first is sometimes of little importance and at other times it is crucial, depending on the dynamics of the couple's problem: for example, if one spouse has an inhibition about *asking* the other for pleasure. If she is so afraid of rejection, so insecure, so guilty that she is heavily involved in giving as opposed to taking some share of pleasure for herself, then I will—after I point this out—ask her to pleasure her husband first. That way she is more likely to be able to relax and abandon herself to her pleasure,

34

Pleasuring—Woman face down

because she has already "paid." On the other hand if a partner is paranoid, and if he feels controlled and demeaned that he must "serve" his wife, that his beautiful erection is not sufficient to stimulate her, then I will—again after *gently* pointing out some of the fallacies of his attitude—suggest that he be the initial receiver. *After* he has been duly caressed, it might be easier for him to give himself to the task of caressing his wife without experiencing anger.)

"You [the man] lie on your stomach. Then I want you [the woman] to caress him as gently and tenderly as you can. Start with the back of his head, his ears, his neck. Go slowly down his back and sides. Down his buttocks, the insides of his thighs. Gently, his legs and his feet. You [the receiver] must try just to concentrate on your feelings. This is very important. Don't worry if she is getting tired or bored. Try to stay with your feeling. And give her feedback. If something feels unpleasant, if she is doing it too fast or too light tell her. If something feels particularly good, tell her or show her.

"When you both have enough of the back turn over. Now do the front the same way. Start with the head and face and neck. Slowly and gently with as much sensitivity as you can find, caress his chest, belly, sides, but not the penis this time. Do the thighs, legs, and feet. Do it till he and you have enough. Then it is your turn. Now you [to the other] do her the same way. Skip the nipples and clitoris and vaginal entrance. Just concentrate on caressing the rest of the body. Any questions? Either of you?"

Reactions to Pleasuring

It is very important to evaluate both partners response to pleasuring in detail and depth. The next therapeutic session usually starts with an inquiry about their experience. Couples are likely to respond briefly: "It was great," "It didn't work," and so on. That is insufficient. A detailed discussion which clarifies the actual experiences of both must be elicited in order for therapy to proceed rationally. In addition, there is a therapeutic value in an open discussion of such feeling as it begins to facilitate authentic communication between the couple.

All behavioral prescriptions elicit *emotions* of which the partners may have varying degrees of awareness. These emotions in turn motivate certain patterns of behavior.

An open probing discussion of the experience helps clarify the affective as well as the behavioral aspects of the experience to both the therapist and to each partner. In order to evaluate the unconscious meanings of these experiences in addition to getting the partners to describe their behavioral and emotional reactions in detail, I also ask for any dreams or fantasies which they may have had during this period. Dreams and fantasies are an excellent means of getting insight into the unconscious significances of these experiences. It is a matter of judgment how this material is to be used clinically. In some cases I will make profound interpretations; at other times insights into more superficial and supportive material is all that is indicated. In general one is governed in one's clinical transactions by the need to avoid the mobilization of profound threat and resistances in both partners.

POSITIVE RESPONSES

Many couples respond very positively to sensate focus. The experience is deeply pleasurable. Some persons enjoy receiving more than giving and vice versa. Often the bond between the couple is enhanced and they are more tender and loving towards each other. Often couples who have had a positive response come to the next therapeutic session holding hands. Often the spouses are relieved to learn that they can give pleasure to the other with their hands and lips, that they do not have to "produce" an erection or lubricate or have intercourse to please their partner. Usually the experiences are sensuous rather than erotic. Occasionally however, one or both may experience intensely erotic feelings and the couple may "disobey" and proceed to orgasm and/or intercourse "against orders." Such behavior is sometimes a resistance born of anxiety, but sometimes such sexual enthusiasm is a healthy expression of growing freedom. Again only a detailed, clear, gently but persistently probing discussion of the physical and emotional responses of the couple can help the therapist evaluate patient responses.

38

Pleasuring—Man face down

NEGATIVE RESPONSES

When the responses are clearly positive, therapy proceeds to the next behavioral prescription which is indicated for that individual case. Often, however, especially if a significant degree of psychopathology or marital pathology exists, persons have negative responses to sensate focus. Adverse emotional reactions vary in intensity from mild and transient to extremely intense and potentially disorganizing. All of these negative responses must either be resolved or bypassed before treatment can proceed.

Some degree of anxiety or discomfort is frequently elicited by engaging in intimate touching and feeling. This is especially true if such contact has been previously avoided for years, and sex had been primarily orgasm-and-performance-oriented.

Negative emotion may be experienced per se, or it may be expressed by avoidance and rationalizing or obsessive behavior:

We didn't have time to do it more than once.

It is too mechanical.

We did it but found it boring, ticklish, silly, and so forth.

I liked doing it to him, but I felt anxiety when he pleasured me.

I thought her arm was getting tired. I couldn't relax. I thought she would get bored.

When he got an erection I felt I had to bring him to orgasm or he would be frustrated.

I just couldn't keep my mind on it. I kept thinking about the kids and dinner.

I felt awful. I am so fat. I thought he would find me repulsive. I just couldn't let him touch me.

I kept wondering if this should give me an erection.

He is so goddamn clumsy. He tickled me, I didn't like it. He is just a lousy lover.

Do I have to go through all that to get laid? Other women just have orgasms without all that fuss.

Causes of Negative Reactions

The causes of the anxiety and anger which may be elicited by mutual pleasuring are many.

If a person has been deeply injured during his formative years, he may protect himself against further injury with alienating defenses. He becomes detached and *avoids intimacy*. Such a patient may experience profound anxiety and anger if his defenses are threatened by the pleasuring experience which compellingly promotes involvement, intimacy, and love.

Guilt about pleasure in general and sex in particular is ubiquitous in our society. When some persons are caressed and stroked the resulting pleasure evokes guilt, and defenses against such guilt must be resolved in the therapy sessions before such a person can be free to enjoy sex.

Hostility toward a spouse may interfere with giving him/her pleasure. If a person is deeply ambivalent about a relationship; if he/she feels exploited, gypped, trapped; there may be a deep resistance to giving the spouse pleasure so that the *giving* part is abortive, clumsy, or sabotaged in some manner. Other hostile and ambivalent persons do not allow themselves to be aroused by the partner. Arousal to such persons is tantamount to involvement, to which they are essentially resistant.

Fear of rejection is often evoked by sensate focus. Some persons feel unless they are giving they will be rejected. They can't ask for themselves. Such persons are likely to experience obsessive thoughts: they are unattractive, the spouse doesn't like doing this, grocery lists or tax obligations and the like nag while they are being caressed. The therapeutic handling of such obsessive defenses includes confrontation with the anxiety which was experienced, as well as interpretations of its unconscious meaning. Specific behavioral prescriptions may also be helpful. For example, one might instruct the couple that the anxious partner must *ask* for what she desires and that the partner must only do what is specifically asked for. The couple is also instructed to share their feelings and reactions to these transactions. In this manner she learns that she will not be rejected if she "dares" to ask him for something. She learns to take responsibility for her own satisfaction. Again, anxiety and defenses evoked by asking are then dealt with in the therapy sessions.

Although this exercise is specifically structured to insure against failure, the *fear of failure* may nevertheless be evoked by sensate focus. An insecure partner will be afraid that he is clumsy and insensitive and feel hopeless about ever being able to please his partner. Reassurance

Pleasuring—Man face up

and corrective experiences can usually diminish this obstacle to sexual abandonment.

Finally deeply neurotic fears and defenses against sexuality are occasionally elicited by sensate focus. For the male these include unconscious fears of injury if one touches and enjoys a woman's body. Such castration fears have a deep long history in the patient's childhood. Fears of homosexuality and of sadistic and masochistic impulses are also occasionally evoked by the open touching and fondling entailed in the process of sensate focus.

Therapy

A negative response to sensate focus on the part of either partner is an obstacle to further therapy which must be resolved or bypassed.

If the negative response is relatively mild, simple *repetition* of the experience along with an interpretive but essentially supportive and reassuring discussion is very often enough to improve the emotional response.

> Do you think you might have been feeling a bit of anxiety when you had those thoughts about your coronary? It is natural to feel a little ill at ease at first. You never allowed yourself to experience such physical intimacy before.

Deeper anxieties such as fear of injury and terror at intimacy often require interpretive kinds of psychotherapeutic intervention, because a certain degree of *resolution* is necessary in order to permit the sexual response to emerge. Resistance to pleasuring often has its roots in a neurotic fear of sexual functioning. If such is the case, resistances must be worked through for a successful outcome. Sometimes, however, when the *process* of sensate focus, and not the *outcome* (i.e., relief of the sexual symptom) evokes anxiety, it is possible to *bypass* this aspect of the process and proceed with other aspects of the treatment. Thus when a person is anxious about touching and intimacy but does not have severe conflict about sexuality per se, the therapist may choose to skip sensate focus and go on to a more genital-oriented task and still obtain a good result in terms of sexual functioning.

45

4

Sensate Focus II –
Genital Pleasuring

Sensate focus II is usually the next step after sensate focus I, but in some cases treatment may begin with this task. When the couple has successfully experienced mutual pleasuring, or when it is the therapeutic decision to omit or detour this experience, they are instructed in genital pleasuring. This refers to gentle, teasing stimulation of the genitals, the objective of which is to produce arousal, but *not* orgasm:

"I want you to experiment with taking turns giving each other genital pleasure. Do as much of the general body caressing as you need to arouse your partner. Then play with his penis. Play gently with the tip and the shaft and the testicles for a little while. Then go to another part of his body. One which he likes. Caress his belly or ears or thighs. Then get back to his penis. Use your fingers or your lips as you and he please. How do you feel about using your mouth on the genitals?"

(Feelings about oral-genital sex must be dealt with explicitly at some point in therapy. This subject is often intensely invested with emotion and there may be a temptation to avoid this. However it should be confronted or it may become an obstacle to openness and a potential source of anxiety. It is easy for the spouses as well as therapist to be biased in either direction with regard to oral sex. Some persons feel oral sex is disgusting and neurotic and a person who is healthy sexually does not need such "extreme" stimulation. Other prejudices run to the opposite. Some persons feel that oral sex is a necessary prerequisite for a full sex life, that anyone who objects is inhibited and neurotic, and this issue must be resolved in order to have fully satisfactory sex. Actually there is no proof to support either position. Some persons can have

Genital Stimulation—Masters and Johnson position for stimulating the woman's clitoris and vagina

a fully satisfying sex life without oral stimulation. Oral stimulation is certainly *not* a necessary product or process of sex therapy. On the other hand oral sex, both giving and receiving the stimulation, is found exquisitely pleasurable and gratifying by many perfectly normal couples, and sometimes in the course of sex therapy inhibitions to oral sex are resolved with very happy results. The most challenging therapeutic situations are those in which one partner ardently desires oral stimulation and the other is repelled or feels guilty about this sexual technique. Such an impasse often presents opportunities for effective therapeutic intervention whose benefits extend substantially beyond an improvement in sexual functioning.)

"I want you to use a teasing tempo. Do not use the rhythmic, driving stimulation which leads to orgasm. If he gets no erection, that's fine. He will still feel pleasure. If he gets one, play with him for a little while, then caress another part of his body. Don't worry if the erection goes down. That is natural and normal. It will come up again if you don't worry about it. You [to the man] while she is caressing you, try not to become distracted. Stay with your feelings. Enjoy the feelings.

"After you have enough, it is your [to the woman] turn. I want you to play with her whole body first. Then when you feel she is ready, or when she tells you, play with her breasts. Gently kiss and pinch the nipples. Play with the pubic hair around her clitoris. Do not touch the clitoris right away. Play around with the vaginal entrance. Do not put your finger all the way into the vagina. That doesn't feel good to most women. Touch the clitoris lightly. Go somewhere else. Go back to the clitoris. Be as gentle and sensitive as you can. Try [to the woman] to give him a little feedback. He has no possible way of knowing what you are feeling. Men have erections, but our responses are internal. He cannot tell "where you are" unless you tell him. Let him know what feels good. You have to tell him what you are feeling if you want him to give you pleasure. Again [to the man] do *not* at this point use the rubbing, driving kind of rhythmic stimulation which produces orgasm. There is a lot of pleasure in just being touched and aroused. One doesn't have to have an orgasm to have pleasure. There are several positions in which this is comfortable. Some people like the position shown in Figures 5 and 6 others have found 7 and 8 to be particularly good. Other couples prefer to find their own positions."

49

Reactions

Many persons who have sexual difficulties when they attempt to have intercourse or when they are striving for orgasm are able to experience intense erotic pleasure and also to respond physiologically when genital pleasuring is the goal of the interaction. This is not surprising because by structuring the situation in this manner many sources of fear and tension which are produced by intercourse are eliminated. Neither partner has to perform. They are "taking turns," so one's response is not contingent on the other's. When the humane goal of pleasure is substituted for the pressured goal of performance, the sexual situation often becomes relaxed enough for the erotic responses to develop freely. The man becomes excited, and before he knows it has several erections. The woman may feel intense erotic pleasure for the first time in her life, or more commonly for the first time since her precoital "petting" days. She may lubricate and desire intercourse. Again couples may "break training" at this point. And again this may be a healthy or a resistant manifestation depending on the underlying emotion.

When the responses to genital pleasuring are positive one proceeds to the next step in treatment, which may be extracoital orgasm or coitus. As always, prescription is highly individualistic. It is the negative responses, which frequently occur, that represent the therapeutic challenge.

NEGATIVE REACTIONS

Genital pleasuring may evoke special kinds of negative emotional reactions in one or both spouses. Whereas sensate focus is likely to evoke anxiety about intimacy, trust, sensuousness, and feelings associated with a negative body image, genital pleasuring is more likely to evoke specific sexual anxiety. The anxiety may range from mild and transient to severe and phobic. The anxiety and guilt evoked by mutual fondling of genitals may be experienced per se or may become obscured by a myriad of defenses and avoidances. Just how the negative affect is experienced depends on the degree to which the person is in touch with

*Genital Stimulation—Masters and Johnson position for stimulating
the man without erection*

Genital Stimulation—Woman touching man's erect penis

his feelings. If he is not aware that his lack of feelings, his obsessive ruminations while he is being stimulated, the late TV watching which prevents the experience from being carried out, and similar phenomena are expressions of the anxiety evoked by genital play, then this is what I discuss with the couple during the therapy session. How deep the interpretations should be made, how much insight into unconscious sources of anxiety is necessary for sexual functioning to improve is a matter of clinical judgment and personal therapeutic style. I tend to make interpretations on rather deep unconscious levels and balance these with enough support to keep resistances from mobilizing. Other therapists (who also get very good results in therapy) tend to stay on a more superficial "counseling" level in their interpretations.

Thus for example, when a patient complained that he started to think about his business as his wife was caressing his penis, he was confronted with the possibility that this is an obsessive defense against some sort of anxiety.

THERAPIST: What do you suppose might be making you anxious? What were you experiencing when you started to ruminate?

MAN: Well it was feeling good. I started to have a fantasy. . . . then I thought, don't have a fantasy that is bad . . . the doctor said stay with your feelings . . . I don't know . . . I often think of business during sex."

Later it developed that the patient used to guard himself against "impure thoughts" as a young and religious man with school problems. Through interpretation he came to understand that he had harbored intense conflict about masturbation. It was not surprising that the present sexual experience evoked his old guilt and anxiety about masturbation and also the old defenses against this. In the therapeutic sessions his early masturbation was reevaluated in a positive light as a sign of healthy struggle against the efforts of others to suppress his healthy sexuality. This support enabled him to accept and work through his masturbatory guilt. Unless adequately balanced with genuine support this sensitive sort of material may be difficult to handle within a brief therapy since one can hardly rely on a long-standing trusting therapeutic relationship to counterbalance the anxiety mobilized by recognition of threatening unconscious material.

Genital fondling often evokes negative feelings and defenses against the appearance, odors, and secretions of the partner's and the person's own genitals. This material is openly worked through in the therapeutic sessions. These frank discussions of previously taboo and shameful topics are of immense value in improving the communications between, and security of, the couple, above and beyond the immediate goals of sex therapy.

Certain specific negative feelings recur again and again and are typically evoked by genital pleasuring prescriptions. These are guilt about feeling and showing pleasure, covert hostility toward one's partner, and fear of rejection by one's partner. The first two have already been discussed in connection with the negative responses to sensate focus while more will be said of the fear of rejection when the tasks used for the treatment of impotence and frigidity are described. On a deeper neurotic level the castration anxieties, homosexual conflicts, and threatening sadomasochistic impulses, which have already been mentioned in the previous section on sensate focus, may also be elicited by genital touching.

Therapeutic Management

Repetition, insight, or bypass are the three therapeutic strategies which may be employed to manage negative responses to any of the prescribed sexual tasks. This is also true of genital pleasuring.

When anxiety and defenses are mild, mere repetition combined with some interpretation and support are usually sufficient to propel therapy forward.

Go home and try it again. Tell him the way you like him to touch you best and do it again. It is hard to shed the anxieties of a lifetime in just a few weeks. You will probably be more relaxed this time.

56

Genital Stimulation—Man touching woman's nipples

When feelings run deep I try to promote insight. This is possible only if rapport and understanding are sufficiently developed so that interpretations of unconscious material can be made incisive and yet supportive enough to foster insight without mobilizing resistances.

Sometimes when pathology is too tenacious and profound for any reasonable hope at rapid resolution I try to bypass the anxiety. I try to lower the defenses against sexuality, while providing defenses against the associated anxiety.

First, one usually confronts the patient with the fact that obsessive ruminations are a manifestation of anxiety. One admonishes the patient to be temporarily "selfish" and to concentrate solely on his own feelings.

> Be selfish—her turn will come next. You have to abandon yourself to your feelings if you want to function. Everyone does. She does, too.

At this point I often encourage the spouse to talk about her own "selfishness," i.e., her ability to stay with her feelings and her fantasies as her sexual arousal builds up. This does much to liberate the more guilty and controlled spouse.

Another excellent method of bypassing resistances is by suggesting that the patient distract himself with erotic fantasy while he is being stimulated. The use of fantasy as a method of overcoming resistances to sexual abandonment will be dealt with when the orgastic dysfunctions of women and of men are discussed.

Finally resistances can be bypassed by changing the sexual prescription. If his partner's fondling of his genitals arouses too much anxiety in a man, he might be instructed only to caress his partner and bring her to orgasm during the next week. Her arousal together with his growing frustration might be reassuring and stimulating enough to bypass his anxieties and allow him to function.

59

B. Erotic Techniques Used for Specific Dysfunctions

5

Frigidity—Female Sexual Unresponsiveness

The unresponsive woman feels no erotic sensation or sexual pleasure. She does not show the signs of physiological arousal, i.e., she remains relatively dry even though she is stimulated by her partner and has intercourse. Her conscious attitudes towards sex vary. She may loathe sexual activity, feel neutral, or even enjoy the physical contact.

The truly unresponsive woman is rare, and this is fortunate because she is difficult to treat. In our experience general unresponsiveness—particularly when it is primary, i.e., the woman has never been responsive to any man in any situation—has of all the dysfunctions the poorest prognosis with brief sex therapy. The prognosis is much better if the woman has been responsive in other situations but is now unresponsive to her husband. Even in situational frigidity however, extensive psychotherapy is often necessary before the patient is amenable to sex therapy and before sexual functioning can be obtained. Nevertheless, even in this difficult dysfunction, which often requires prior resolution of tenacious unconscious intrapsychic and marital conflict, the prescribed sexual tasks play an important role in therapy.

Sometimes these are not employed until the patient has resolved basic conflicts by means of psychotherapy. At other times the tasks may be used concurrently with psychotherapy in order to facilitate rapid resolution of obstacles which arise during the course of treatment.

Perhaps one can formulate the basic dynamics of unresponsivity as follows: The woman harbors an unconscious conflict about allowing herself sexual pleasure with a man. There does not seem to be one specific conflict in this disorder. It may involve deep oedipal fears of injury, hostility towards men in general or towards the specific man in question, fears of rejection if she "lets go," performance anxiety, erotic guilt, and so forth. The defenses against these conflicts specifically prevent the woman from responding. She either avoids receiving adequate stimulation, or if she doesn't actually prevent her lover from stimulating her, she erects *perceptual defenses* against enjoying this stimulation. She literally does not allow herself any erotic feelings. She unconsciously does not allow herself to respond. She prevents herself from abandoning herself to the sexual experience.

Treatment Strategy

The basic strategy in therapy is to attempt to structure the sexual situation so that the woman is able to respond to adequate and heightened sexual stimulation while she is in a relaxed, nonanxious and loving state. Under such conditions, she must learn to resensitize herself to the sensations she has defensively suppressed for a long time. Again the creation of a tranquil sexual system between the partners often requires considerable psychotherapeutic intervention but with this in mind, the following is a typical (but not universal) sequence of events which we employ at the Cornell Sex Therapy Clinic to treat the generally unresponsive female.

1. Sensate focus I
2. Sensate focus II
3. Nondemand coitus
4. Coitus to orgasm

Among this group of patients there is a very high prevalence of negative responses to the sensate focus exercises. These reactions are of course incorporated into the psychotherapeutic process. In addition to the psychotherapeutic explorations, when the history reveals that the woman experienced high levels of arousal in precoital and pre-marital "petting" situations, we might initially prescribe such activity while the couple is clothed, instead of the traditional nude and more exposed and therefore more threatening, pleasuring.

Nondemand Coitus

This exercise is optimally employed after the woman has shown a positive response to the sensate focus exercises which were described in the previous chapters. However, if genital touching arouses insurmountable resistance, it may occasionally be bypassed and nondemand coitus introduced at this time.

The couple is told to caress each other until the man has a good erection and until the woman has some degree of lubrication. If she fails to respond with adequate vasocongestion he is instructed to lubricate his penis with petroleum jelly.

Then the woman mounts in the superior position. She inserts his penis into her vagina. She allows it to rest there for a little while, while she gets the "feel" of the erect phallus in her vagina. She contracts the pubococcygeal muscles against his penis, again to acquaint herself with the vaginal feelings of which such women are often not aware. Then she starts to slowly move up and down on her husband's erect phallus. She plays and experiments with different motions and excursions. She should be moved solely by her own feelings and *not* by a regard for him. She must *temporarily* suspend her usual concern for his pleasure. She must be temporarily "selfish" so she can learn to feel her vaginal sensations.

He lends his erect penis and his gentle encouragement to the enterprise. If he should become too excited, he indicates this, and the couple "rests" for a while. This can be done with the penis inside the vagina or he can withdraw and later, after he has regained control, he can re-enter. The in-and-out interrupted coitus has a teasing effect which often heightens the woman's arousal.

62

Female superior—nondemanding thrusting

During the rest periods, the couple may be instructed to desist from stimulation. In other cases he stimulates her clitoris during the rest from intromission. In still other cases she is instructed to stimulate herself during these times.

The end of the exercise is reached when she is tired or when she has an orgasm, [which is exceedingly *unusual,* especially in the early phases of therapy]. More commonly they stop when she feels tired and satisfied that she has learned some additional vaginal sensations. Sometimes the man's ejaculatory urge becomes insistent and he does not wish to continue without climax. At any rate, at the termination of the exercise the man is usually provided with an orgasm, either by thrusting to orgasm on coitus, or by extravaginal stimulation.

It should be noted that even a well functioning, normal male may lose his erection during the course of the nondemand sexual exercises. This is no cause for concern for the male can easily be stimulated to another erection. The important subject of regaining lost erections is dealt with in the chapter on erectile dysfunction.

It is clear from the foregoing description that the nondemand coital exercises require the active cooperation of a functional male partner. He must have some degree of "erectile security" as well as good ejaculatory control. This is a good example of why sex therapy requires the participation of a cooperative couple, even when the partner has in no way caused or perpetuated his mate's sexual difficulty.

REACTIONS TO NONDEMAND COITUS

Women's reactions run the gamut from great pleasure and excitement and occasionally even orgasm—through a desired increase in vaginal sensations, erotic pleasure, and loving feelings—to the negative responses of anesthesia or to profoundly disturbing emotional reactions.

Male responses to this exercise also cover a wide spectrum. Some men are delighted to provide an erect phallus to help their wive's with their difficulty. They take pleasure and pride as well as sexual gratification from the experience. Other men have negative reactions—

anxiety and/or anger—to this previously avoided situation wherein the woman assumes control of the sexual interaction and is extremely active and "selfish." Again, these reactions reveal extremely valuable material for psychotherapeutic exploration.

When the reactions are positive the couple proceeds to regular coitus. If not, the negative reactions must first be worked through.

Many women who have sexual inhibitions are overconcerned with their partner's gratification to the neglect of their own. One must differentiate between the desirable qualities of generosity—sensitivity to one's lover and concern for his feelings—and the neurotic, immature, and compulsive neglect of one's own feelings, in the anxiety to please and serve. The latter is essentially a masochistic pattern of relating to the opposite gender. It is born of deep anxiety. Usually a masochistic person has profound feelings of inadequacy and self-loathing. She can not really believe that an attractive man can love her and accept her if she is merely herself: her sexual, emotional, real self. She must constantly serve and please and give him pleasure. She must not relax and enjoy herself. Such a person, whether female *or* male, has great difficulties in abandoning themselves to their erotic pleasures. It has been repeatedly emphasized that a substantial degree of abandonment is a prerequisite of sexual functioning.

The partner often unconsciously is attracted to and subtly perpetuates his wife's masochism. He permits her to serve, give pleasure, gratify him. This may allow a basically insecure man to function with a minimum of anxiety.

Some degree of sexual masochism, not in the extreme sense of being aroused by injury or physical violence, but rather in the form of sexual self-sacrifice, is very common in our male-oriented culture. We are taught from early childhood that sexual pleasure is the male's due. The woman must make herself as attractive and pleasing as possible. It is all right for her to have some pleasure too, but only really in the service of his. Beyond this cultural masochism, however, nonresponsive women often tend to be psychologically masochistic and compulsively giving—unable to ask or take. These insecurities spring from destructive and incorrectly perceived childhood experiences and neurotic adaptations to these.

66

It is not surprising that when unconscious masochistic patterns which serve one or both partners' deep unconscious needs are revealed by a structured behavioral task designed to give *control* to the woman, to govern the activity by *her* needs, to *neglect* the man's gratification, no matter how temporarily—a great deal of anxiety and defenses against this anxiety are evoked. Indeed, the nondemand coital exercises frequently provoke anxiety and deep insecurities in women and sometimes in the husband as well.

Management of such resistance consists of repetition of the task and active, vigorous psychotherapy. This is designed to reveal and resolve the self-destructive sexual behavior and most importantly also to correct the low self-esteem which often lies at its roots. In addition it is extremely important to be alert to any reciprocal psychopathology on the part of the husband. Some husbands and lovers of masochistic women do not have an unconscious investment in their wives' lack of pleasure. They really would be much happier if their wives were responsive. Others, however, because of their own insecurities derive some unconscious gratification from the lover's masochism. In such cases this dynamic must be dealt with or the partner is likely to sabotage the treatment. This can be done either by bypass or resolution. Bypass in such cases is psychotherapeutic and not strictly behavioral. For intercourse of course cannot be bypassed in most dysfunctional cases treated with sex therapy. When a sadomasochistic pattern is too tenacious to yield to brief intervention, bypass may consist of subtly communicating to the couple that they can retain the essential features of their psychological interactions, but at the same time they can still function sexually. They can fight and struggle if they must, but they can keep their neurotic interactions out of the bedroom.

Partner rejection is another common underlying cause for unresponsiveness in women, especially when this dysfunction is situational. Some persons can dissociate their sexual and affectionate responses to a great degree. They can enjoy and function in sexual experiences even when they have a detached or even a negative emotional connection to their partner. Other persons, especially women, cannot. Some unresponsive women who seek sex therapy are not aware that they are deeply angry or at least ambivalent towards their husbands. They feel

67

exploited, cheated, and angry, and yet may be entirely unaware of their hostile feelings. Nevertheless these feelings inhibit their sexual responses to their husbands. At times partner rejection can be bypassed behaviorally, and the woman can learn to respond sexually in spite of her ambivalence. In other cases, the anger poses an insurmountable obstacle to sexual responsiveness and must be resolved psychotherapeutically before the patient can respond to the sexual exercises. Similar considerations apply to deep unconscious sexual conflicts which derive from oedipal problems and guilt about sexual pleasure which are also prevalent obstacles to female sexual responsiveness.

Orgasm

When the nondemanding, teasing coital exercises produce erotic responsiveness in the woman, the couple is instructed to proceed with ordinary coitus designed to lead to orgasm in both partners. Sometimes this produces orgasm in the woman. Other times it does not and other techniques designed to facilitate orgasm are prescribed.

Usually one does not specifically attempt to foster the unresponsive patient's orgastic response in the initial phases of therapy. It is the aim of this phase of treatment to enhance her general responsiveness. A goal oriented, orgasm-achieving orientation paradoxically is sometimes an obstacle rather than an aid to therapy. In some cases however, when the patient's unresponsiveness is secondary to repeated attempts and failures to reach orgasm, orgastic exercises are prescribed. These are described in the next chapter on the orgastic dysfunctions.

In unresponsive women with very low libido one tries to enhance her sexual response by other than tactile means. Low levels of testosterone, fantasy, and erotic literature have all been used to implement this objective.

PUBOCOCCYGEUS MUSCLE EXERCISES

Dr. Arnold Kegel has claimed that weakness and disuse of the pubococcygeus muscle is a factor in female unresponsiveness. He and his

68

Male inside female from rear—touching her clitoris

followers prescribe pubococcygeal muscle exercises. The effectiveness of this practice has not yet been evaluated systematically. However there is a certain rationale for this procedure and hence it is used by many sex therapists.

Essentially, proprioceptive sensations from the perivaginal muscles are an important source of pleasurable erotic vaginal sensation. Also the female orgasm consists of contraction of the ischio cavernosii, bulbo cavernosii and pubococcygeus muscles. Therefore, the reasoning is that strengthing the tone of these muscles would be helpful in producing stronger and more enjoyable orgasms.

If these muscles are found to be lax and atrophic on vaginal examination, or just on an empirical basis, the patient is directed to contract her pubococcygens muscles 10 times once or twice each day. If she has no awareness of these muscles she is told to start and stop her stream of urine. It is the pubococcygeus muscles which are contracted in the process of stopping the stream of urine. Thereby the patient learns to be aware of this group of muscles. The muscles can be exercised during routine daily chores.

An instrument called the perineometer enables a woman to contract her pubococcygens muscles against resistance which is measured by manometer via a device inserted into her vagina. Few sex therapists employ such an elaborate procedure.

6

Female Orgastic Dysfunction

A clear distinction should be made between the totally unresponsive woman and the woman who *is* responsive, enjoys erotic feeling, has a good vasocongestive response, but who has difficulties to varying degrees in achieving orgasm. In the past both were included under the rubric of "frigidity" and were considered to be a single disorder. This is an error, because while both syndromes have much in common and overlap to a certain extent, they are the product of different underlying mechanisms and respond to somewhat different treatment procedures.

The definition of orgastic dysfunction is a subject of controversy because the normal range and limits of the female orgasmic response has not yet been defined.

The orgasm is a reflex. All reflexes have a range and distribution of thresholds. In other words some persons need only a mild tap on the knee to elicit a kick, others will not respond until they receive a good sharp bang on the patellar tendon. Both are perfectly normal, i.e., the neural apparatus which mediates the reflex is intact. There is a normal *range* in the threshold of the patellar reflex. The thresholds of reflexes are also influenced by other factors such as psychological inhibition, drugs, and emotional states. Thus a nervous patient may have to be distracted by clasping his hands before the examining physician can elicit the knee jerk. These same considerations apply to the female orgastic reflex. However, we do not know where the normal limits of this important reflex lie.

Clinically, female orgasm seems to be distributed more or less along a bell-shaped curve. On one extreme are the women who have never climaxed at all. Next are women who require intense clitoral stimulation when they are alone and not "disturbed" by a partner. Women who need direct clitoral stimulation but are able to climax with their partners fall in the middle range. Also near the middle are women who can climax on coitus but only after lengthy and vigorous stimulation. Near the upper range are women who require only brief penetration to reach their climax and at the very extreme are the women who can achieve an orgasm via fantasy and/or breast stimulation alone.

Everyone agrees on criteria of normalcy and pathology at the extreme ends of the orgastic continuum. Clearly the woman who is totally anorgastic—i.e., the woman who has never had an orgasm at all—is inhibited and in the need of treatment. It is also clear that the woman who is rapidly and easily orgastic on coitus is normal. The controversy pertains to the middle range in the spectrum of female orgastic threshold.

Some workers in the field, including myself, consider women who are orgastic on clitoral stimulation when they are with their partners as normal. Others consider any woman who is not coitally orgastic, even though she is highly responsive and multiply orgastic on clitoral stimulation in the presence of a partner, as frigid. There is at this time insufficient data available to settle this controversy definitively.

On an empirical basis, until we have definitive evidence, we proceed as follows. We treat all women who complain of orgastic difficulty, coital or absolute. The totally anorgastic woman presents a special clinical problem. Such patients have an excellent prognosis for learning to have orgasms with sex therapy. We also accept coitally inorgastic women for treatment because they also can often benefit from therapy. For some women clitoral stimulation seems to be their normal response pattern and they and their husbands merely need counseling and reassurance to this effect. For other women, however, the lack of coital orgasm is indeed a product of inhibition or poor technique, and this segment of the patient population often learns to achieve the desired goal of coital orgasm with sex therapy. These two varieties of the orgastic dysfunctional syndrome, the total anorgastic and the situationally inorgastic woman, present somewhat different clinical problems and are therefore dealt with in separate sections.

73

Treatment Strategy

In general the basic treatment plan for orgasmic dysfunction is:

1. orgasm alone (masturbation)
2. orgasm with the partner—on clitoral stimulation
3. orgasm on intercourse

If orgasm on intercourse does not occur:
1. bridge maneuver

A—The Totally Inorgastic Woman

Approximately 8 percent of females in the United States have never had an orgasm. Some of these women are inorgastic because they have never been stimulated properly, others cannot respond with orgasm to even the most intense stimulation. For a variety of reasons these women have learned to inhibit their orgasmic reflex. This inhibition is entirely involuntary and such women often ardently desire the orgasmic experience.

MASTURBATION

The main principle of achieving orgasm is simple: maximize the stimulation and minimize the inhibition. To minimize inhibiting factors, it is often best to have the woman stimulate herself to orgasm when she is alone and free from the pressure of being observed and "timed" by her partner. To do this one must often help her resolve guilt and shame about masturbation. This is done during the therapy sessions.

Women who have never experienced orgasm are confused about the experience. Often they are frightened and anticipate injury. Such patients are asked to talk about their fantasies about orgasm. What do they think will happen? Women have varying degrees of awareness

74

Female alone masturbating with finger

about their fearful orgasmic fantasies. These must be explored in the sessions, and it is often useful to discuss their genesis in a reasonable and supportive manner. Some common fears which center around punishment for sexual pleasure include: "I will lose control," "I will go crazy," "It will injure me—I will get cancer—die—and so forth," "I will love it and become wildly promiscuous," "I must be in love before I can have an orgasm." Most of such fantasies clearly have their roots in childhood prohibitions against sexuality. Dreams and associations are often useful in working through such unconscious impediments to orgasmic release. And the patient must be reassured on the deepest level about the unrealistic nature of her injury fantasies.

At other times, if a woman is guilty about pleasure and success she may have the opposite fantasy—that orgasm represents the ultimate in success. In such cases she has to be reassured that orgasm is *not* the ultimate transcendental experience which will make her supremely happy. When she realizes that her other problems will not be dispelled by her achieving a climax, *then* it is sometimes possible for her to achieve her first orgasm. Ideally of course the basic success conflict should be worked through. This is a lengthy process but in sex therapy it is sometimes possible to confront the patient with this destructive dynamic and take the first steps toward its resolution.

Realistic understanding of orgasm is therapeutic. So I usually describe orgasm to the woman who has never experienced one:

It is a reflex, like a sneeze, only it is much more pleasurable. Orgasm varies very widely in how enjoyable it is, however. Sometimes it is really a great experience and you sort of get totally absorbed in it. Sometimes it is just a pleasant local sensation. Orgasm is a series of pleasurable contractions. There is no mistaking the sensation. It is unique, and you will definitely *know* when you have had an orgasm. When your sexual tension builds up, then there are suddenly some rhythmic contractions of the muscles in your vagina. Those contractions are the pleasurable part. You feel erotic pleasure in your clitoris as you build up to orgasm, but during the contractions you feel the pleasure around the vagina and deep in your pelvis. Sometimes you feel like thrusting

77

your pelvis back and forth when you feel an orgasm coming on. That feels very good. But at other times you are moved to hold quite still and just enjoy the orgastic rush quietly. That also feels very good. You never really lose control or consciousness during an orgasm, but, as I said, sometimes you really can get lost in the cascade of pleasurable sensation. Do you have any questions about this?

After guilt feelings and fears and fantasies and misinformation about orgasm have been dispelled in the therapeutic session, the patient is advised to go home and try out digital masturbation. At this juncture her *erotic fantasies* are explored during the therapeutic sessions. It is important to reassure patients that fantasies, whatever their nature, are normal and indeed very useful in sexual functioning. They serve concomitantly to stimulate and to distract from anxiety. If the patient has sexual fantasies and daydreams she is encouraged to immerse herself in these images while she stimulates herself. If she is bereft of erotic fantasies, she is advised to purchase erotic literature and read it as a *probe,* i.e., to see what sort of scene or situation or picture or fantasy will stimulate her. Digital stimulation of the clitoris plus distraction by fantasy often produce orgasm within a few weeks. If it does not, the use of a *vibrator* is suggested. There are several suitable vibrators available for the purpose of female masturbation. The phallus-shaped battery powered machines are *not* good for producing orgasm because the vibrations are not strong enough, while almost any commercial *electric massager,* widely available in drug stores, can be effective.

It is suggested to the patient that she experiment with the vibrator by moving it around and near her clitoral area. Again she is advised to immerse herself in fantasy during the stimulation in order "to distract the distractor," i.e., distract herself from her own tendencies to exert conscious control over her orgastic response. In some cases she may be advised to read erotic literature or observe erotic pictures while she is in the very act of stimulating herself.

Some patients must stimulate themselves for long periods of time, occasionally up to *one hour* before they release into orgasm. The therapist's encouragement is important during this period.

78

Female masturbating with vibrator—male is present

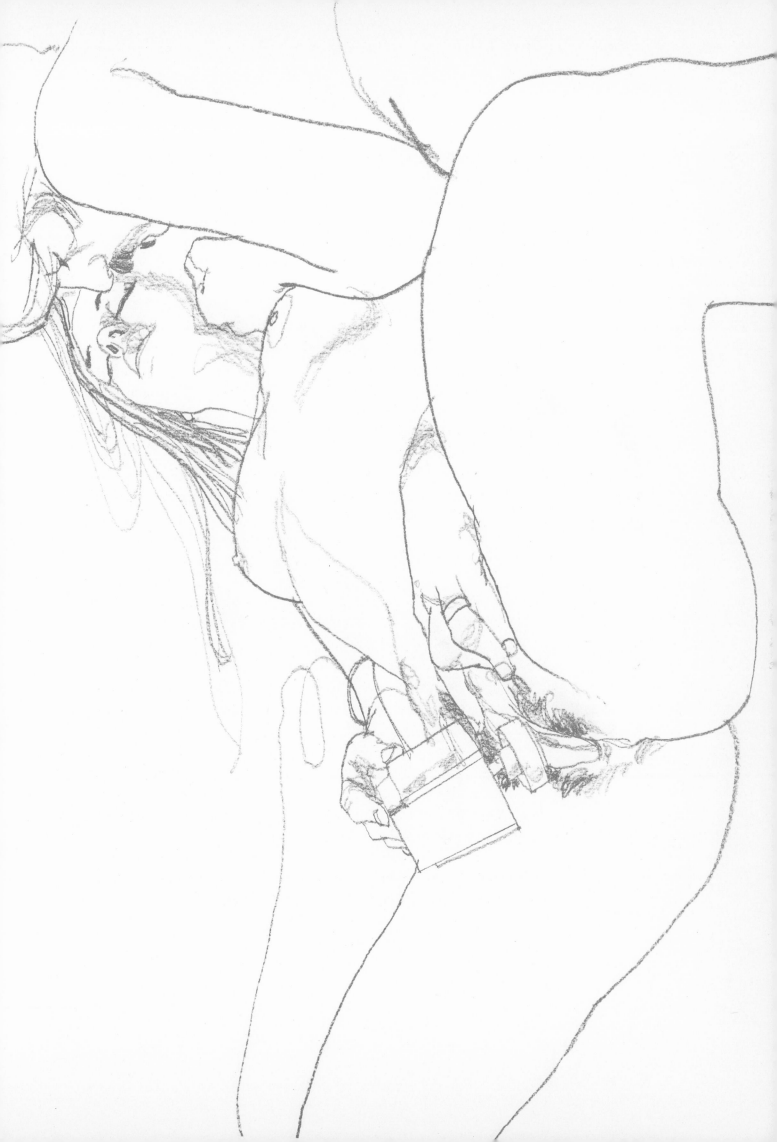

There are several "tricks" or methods which may facilitate orgastic release. It helps some women to "bear down" when they feel orgasm by alternately tightening and relaxing the vaginal perineal muscles. A method which helps other patients is to thrust their pelvis actively and breathe pantingly at high levels of excitement.

Sometimes when a woman's orgastic response is inhibited, unpleasant tensions and sensations are produced when she is stimulated intensely. At such times it is best to advise her to cease stimulation for a second or so, then to resume again. Several repetitions of this "stop–start" technique often produce the initial orgasm.

All these mechanical techniques probably facilitate orgasm by distracting the woman from her inhibitory tendencies. Again a highly useful "distractor" is an erotic fantasy.

ORGASM WITH THE PARTNER

Reaching an orgasm on masturbation is a wonderful achievement for a woman who has never climaxed, but it is hardly a satisfactory end point of treatment. After a woman can reliably masturbate to orgasm alone, the next step in treatment is to have her have an orgasm in the presence of her husband. This is much harder to do because even though it is usually much more stimulating to be with a man than alone with one's fantasies, it is usually also far more anxiety-provoking. One has to perform, produce: "Will I be able to reach a climax? Will he get sick and tired of the tedious stimulation? Are other women quicker?"

There are various techniques to accomplish this next step. For one the couple may be advised to make love in their usual manner. After he climaxes, he stimulates her to orgasm manually. She is advised to use the same mental devices by which she was able to facilitate her orgasm on self-stimulation. She contracts her muscles, breathes pantingly, and above all immerses herself in her favorite fantasies while he stimulates her. This method often produces orgasm in the woman. Gradually it becomes less difficult and gradually she needs less and less fantasy as a distractor.

81

At other times self-masturbation in the presence of the husband is prescribed. This is indicated if the woman is very slow or if she has not yet worked through her reticence at asking for and accepting pleasure from him. Some couples are free enough to accept such a suggestion. Most often, however, women are embarrassed and ashamed and expect rejection from their husbands should they masturbate in his presence. Some husbands are indeed "put off" by this idea. But they are in the minority. Most often to the wife's surprise the husband does not react with the anticipated shock or disgust to his wife's masturbation. To the contrary, he is often intensely excited by the idea. Actually female masturbation is an exceedingly common theme in the erotic fantasies of normal men.

The experience of being open enough to stimulate oneself in the presence of one's mate most often has a salutary effect. It adds yet another dimension of depth and openness to the couple's sexual relationship.

B—The Coitally Inorgastic Woman

Failure to reach orgasm on coitus is the most common sexual complaint of women. This is not surprising when female anatomy and physiology are considered realistically. Experimental and clinical evidence indicates that the female orgasm is a reflex the motor expression of which consists of contractions of muscles surrounding the vagina, although it is triggered by sensory stimulation around the clitoral area. From a mechanical standpoint intercourse is actually a rather poor and indirect way of stimulating the clitoral area.

This point often evokes an intense emotional response from clinicians who for understandable psychological reasons would prefer that vaginal penetration were the best orgasm-producing stimulus. But unfortunately this is not so. Psychologically intercourse produces a highly arousing and emotionally satisfying erotic stimulus. Mechanically, however, clitoral stimulation during intercourse is limited to the traction on the clitoral hood produced by the thrusting phallus, and some pressure around the clitoral area by the man's pubic bone in some

82

Male stimulating female's clitoris manually

Male stimulating female's clitoris orally

positions. This is not as strong a stimulus as direct manipulation of the clitoris. Given these facts it might be predicted that only women with a relatively low orgasmic threshold could reach climax on coitus alone, without any added clitoral stimulation. And indeed although definitive data is missing on this point, according to Fisher's surveys and estimates only one third to one half of women in the United States prefer to reach climax regularly on intercourse. It may be speculated that some of those who do not are not pathologically inhibited. Physiologically these women require more intense clitoral stimulation than is provided by intercourse. Others in this group most probably do represent a truly dysfunctional group. They probably have high orgastic thresholds because of psychological inhibition. The first group of physiologically, coitally anorgastic women need reassurance and counseling. The truly dysfunctional group often benefit from sex therapy.

THE BRIDGE MANEUVER

Sensate focus I and II and nondemand coitus are often used in the initial stages of therapy for coitally inorgastic women. The crucial task for this problem however entails the combination of clitoral stimulation and coitus, a technique which is called "the bridge maneuver." This technique is indicated for the woman who is clitorally responsive and who does not reach orgasm on coitus, but who wishes to do so.

Most coitally inorgastic women who are orgastic on clitoral stimulation can climax if they are stimulated at the same time the penis is contained in the vagina. Women often like techniques which provide such stimulation because the orgastic experience is quite distinct and highly pleasurable if the erect penis is in the vagina at the time of climax. However, use of this technique as a permanent adaptation has the disadvantage of being tedious for the husband. Also this practice seldom leads on to true coital orgasm. The bridge maneuver is different in that the basic idea is to provide the woman with clitoral stimulation *up* to the point of, but not actually to, orgasm, and then let coital thrusting trigger off the orgastic reflex. This is a "bridge" between clitoral stimulation and coitus.

Clitoral stimulation may be provided by the man or by the woman herself, depending on the dynamics of the case. If no specific psychological obstacles exist, there are advantages to advise the woman to stimulate herself, at least during the initial trials of the bridge. Her husband is less likely to find this tedious if stimulation takes a long time, he is apt to become more aroused when he is inside a woman who is stimulating herself, and finally the woman is often more able to relax and concentrate on her pleasure when she is in control of stimulation, and does not have to worry about "his arm getting tired," i.e., being rejected.

There are several positions wherein concomitant clitoral stimulation and intromission can be conducted with comfort. Side to side and woman superior and man kneeling are illustrated in the text in figures 15, 16, and 17. In addition, couples are encouraged to experiment on their own. The important principles in the positions to be used for the "bridge maneuver" are that there be free access for the stimulating hand to clitoris, and that the woman's hips be free for thrusting against the man's pubic bone.

This exercise should be used *after* the woman has experienced enhanced vaginal sensations. Methods to accomplish this include manual stimulation of the sensitive entrance to the vagina and the nondemand coitus exercises which were described in the preceding section.

There are two sources of erotic sensation in the vagina: tactile and proprioceptive. The inner two thirds of the vagina is not invested with touch fibers and is essentially anesthetic. However the entrance and outer one third is exquisitely receptive to touch and gentle manipulation of these areas causes exquisite pleasure in the receptive woman.

Muscle sensations supply another dimension of erotic sensibility. Vaginal muscle contractions can be experienced as intensely pleasurable during thrusting and during the orgastic contractions. The slow nondemanding coital thrusting which was described in the foregoing section along with pubococcygeal muscle exercises are useful in enhancing the vaginal sensations of some women who have defensively suppressed these perceptions in the past. Sometimes when vaginal sensations have been enhanced by these techniques, the woman spontaneously experiences coital orgasm. Most often however she does not and the bridge maneuver is then prescribed.

88

Bridge—male stimulating female's clitoris while he is inside

Bridge—female stimulating her own clitoris while male is inside

Directions for the bridge maneuver may be given as follows: "Play with each other in your usual way, until you [man] have a good erection, and until you [woman] feel quite aroused and desire to be entered. Then you enter her in the side-to-side, woman superior or kneeling, and so forth position." (The preferred position should be explored and described with the couple. Pictures are very helpful here.)

"While you [to the man] are inside, thrust slowly, with just enough rhythm and depth to maintain your erection. If you hold still altogether you may lose your erection. But do not thrust too intrusively. I want her to concentrate on her stimulation. In the meantime you [woman] stimulate your clitoris with your finger, just as you do when you are by yourself." (Directions can be varied so that the man stimulates the woman. This should only be done if she is easily orgasmic on his manipulation. Also a vibrator may be used for the bridge maneuver. Actually this is a highly effective means of promoting female orgasm during bridging. Its disadvantage lies only in that some couples object to this mechanical means of stimulation during coitus.)

"Concentrate on your favorite fantasy while you are being stimulated, just as you do when you are alone. When you feel orgasm coming on, *stop* the stimulation and actively thrust. This interruption may bring you 'down,' i.e., it may stop rather than trigger your orgasm. That is to be expected. Don't worry. Do it again. Hold still with your husband's penis inside and stimulate yourself to the point of orgasm. When it feels like it's just before, *stop*. Thrust fast and hard against him. You may have to repeat this several times before it works. If you [the man] get too stimulated to hold out, proceed to orgasm. That is natural. This can be a very exciting experience. You can try the bridge again next time you have sex. How do you feel about this assignment?"

REACTIONS TO THE BRIDGE

The bridge is often successful in allowing women to experience coital orgasm. Usually the couple's response to this is relief and enthusiasm, often to euphoric intensity. Women who have never experienced coital orgasm often feel very frustrated and tend to overvalue this experience. Often they feel inferior to women who can climax on intercourse. If they are insecure and do not value themselves as persons, they may develop paranoid defenses and may even fear that their lovers will abandon them and seek a woman who is coitally orgasmic. And indeed men also may have an intense emotional response to the coital anorgasticity of their wives. Insecure men in particular are apt to fear there is something inadequate in themselves if his partner doesn't climax "by his penis." Or they may project this anxiety and insecurity onto their wives and interpret this pattern of sexual response to mean that she is "sick" or expressing her hostility by "holding out."

For these reasons there is high prevalence of coital orgasmic simulation in our society. Women find it easier to forego orgasm and pretend, rather than to admit openly their clitoral pattern of responsiveness. The admission of truth on the part of the wife after many years of pretending to reach climax is often the initial and crucial step in the therapy of this condition.

The bridge maneuver almost always yields coital orgasm except when a woman has a specific and tenacious conflict about penetration. However the bridge does not progress to easy coital orgasm in all cases. Exact data are lacking on the outcome of this treatment for this complaint. In our experience fewer than half of coitally anorgastic women treated by this means become progressively more easily orgastic on intercourse to the point where they no longer require any clitoral "priming" to reach orgasm. The rest have learned a good technique for reaching orgasm with the penis inside, one which is potentially pleasurable for both partners. However these women continue to require some degree of direct clitoral stimulation before they climax.

When a woman remains essentially coitally anorgastic, the couple is in need of sexual counseling. Sometimes they easily accept this as a good and normal pattern of female sexual responsiveness. At other times, deeply emotional attitudes about coital orgasm must be worked through psychodynamically before a couple can relax enough to enjoy their sexual interactions on a realistic basis.

Orgasm is really highly pleasurable no matter how it occurs, providing neither partner considers noncoital orgasm as "second best."

94

Bridge—male is kneeling—female is stimulating herself
with vibrator while male is inside

Secure and loving couples can have gloriously fulfilling sex lives even though the woman requires clitoral stimulation in order to climax.

The process of sex therapy for female sexual problems does not consist solely of mechanical exercises. It entails some striking changes of attitudes on the part of the woman. She must learn to accept her own sexual needs and wishes for erotic pleasure as a good thing and not just as a means of pleasing her husband. She must take responsibility for her own sexual gratification, i.e., she must actively make sure she is adequately stimulated and not depend entirely on her man's sensitivity and generosity. In practical terms this means that a woman who has always had intercourse in response to signals from her husband, who was largely moved by her husband's erotic needs, pace, and wishes, now sits astride in the female superior position and slowly moves upon his erect phallus according to the demands of *her* vaginal sensations!

Not surprisingly this move from passivity to activity may evoke intense emotions from the male partner. Some men, who are basically secure and loving, are relieved and delighted. Other men are deeply threatened and made angry by their wives' activity and growing strength. These changes may mobilize fears of being controlled and even injured by a powerful female. In analytic terms old oedipal and castration anxieties may be aroused in the man by the woman's more assertive role. Some are aware of these feelings and express them openly. Others are not in touch but suddenly become impotent or disinterested in sex.

It has been my experience that usually, if he is not deeply disturbed, the husband of a previously unresponsive or anorgastic woman who now becomes a more active participant in the sexual interaction can accept this and ultimately benefits in terms of his own sexuality. It is more gratifying for most persons of either gender to make love to a responsive partner who both actively stimulates and seeks stimulation— one who gently initiates sex and who expresses enjoyment. However the sexual system may be temporarily disjointed by the woman's transition to sexual maturity and the therapist must be careful to support the couple during the adjustment period. Activity must be differentiated from demand; initiation from aggression; the gentle expression of a wish from criticism.

97

SHE: I only said I would enjoy his kissing my breasts and he got mad.

HE: She is always putting down my lovemaking. I don't need instructions.

THERAPIST: Wouldn't you [to him] like to know what especially pleases her?

HE: Of course.

THERAPIST: How can she tell you without offending you? Tell her— now.

Successful resolution of female sexual difficulties depends on *both* partner's acceptance without guilt or shame or anxiety of her erotic needs and wishes. The husband's negative attitude, his inability to accept his wife's sexual autonomy may prove an obstacle to her sexual fulfillment which must be resolved during the course of therapy.

7

Vaginismus

Vaginismus is a disorder in which sexual intercourse is not possible because attempts at vaginal penetration evoke an involuntary spastic contraction of the vaginal entrance. This is a relatively rare condition. Response to sex therapy is excellent.

Evidence suggests that the essential pathology of this condition is a conditioned reaction of the muscles which guard the vaginal introitus. Apparently these muscles are readily conditionable to respond with intense spasm. The unconditioned stimulus responsible for the acquisition of the vaginismic response can be any source of pain associated with penetration. Physical disease, psychologically painful affect such as conscious or unconscious fear and/or guilt, traumatic sexual assaults all have been associated with the acquisition and perpetuation of vaginismus. Sometimes the traumatic source cannot be identified.

Vaginismus must be differentiated from physical obstructions of the vaginal entrance and also from simple phobic avoidance of penetration. The diagnosis of vaginismus can only be made on pelvic examination.

Treatment Strategy

Treatment essentially consists of extinction of the conditioned vaginal response. This is accomplished by the introduction, under relaxed and tranquil conditions, of objects of gradually increasing size into the vaginal entrance. When the patient can tolerate a phallus size object, she is cured.

This incredibly simple treatment plan is complicated by the fact that

99

most vaginismic women do not present with a simple conditioned reflex which closes their vaginas. These women usually are also *phobic* of intercourse and penetration. The phobic avoidance must be dispelled before the deconditioning part of treatment can commence.

There are various techniques for managing phobic avoidance of intercourse. These include analytic interpretation of the unconscious elements which underlie the irrational fear; support and reassurance and encouragement to "stay with the fearful feelings" and attempt penetration in spite of these feelings; and such behavioral techniques as systematic desensitization and hypnosis. I generally employ an amalgam of the analytic and supportive methods. I try to explore the original source or trauma which led to the establishment of the vaginismus and work through the emotional responses to this. I quickly go beyond its genesis into the here-and-now destructive effects of the problem and support the patient's constructive and rational efforts to overcome this. However, others have used the more strictly behavioral approaches with reportedly good results.

In-vivo desensitization or insertion begins only after the woman's phobic avoidance of vaginal penetration has been diminished and after her ambivalences towards intercourse have been resolved sufficiently so that she is relatively free of conflict about the procedure. Clinicians use a variety of objects to be inserted into the vagina for deconditioning. Some recommend graduated glass catheters, others use rubber, and still others use a tampon. It is irrelevant for the purpose of conditioning what the nature of the object is. I use the patient's and the husband's finger only because I have found this to be most emotionally acceptable to patients and therefore less likely to mobilize therapeutic resistances than artificial objects.

Procedure

The patient is instructed to observe her vaginal entrance in a mirror while she is by herself. She is told to place her index finger at the vaginal entrance and see what it feels like to insert her finger tip into the vaginal entrance. These feelings and their meanings are explored in the

Female inserting her own finger into vagina

Female inserting catheter into vagina

Male inserting his finger into woman's vagina

Male inserting an object into woman's vagina

subsequent therapy session in a reassuring manner. In addition discussion of any dreams and fantasies which the patient may have during this period are frequently helpful in revealing and resolving the unconscious forces which in some cases serve to perpetuate the conditioned reflex.

When the patient can insert a finger tip, she is told next time to insert her entire finger. Then two fingers. Sometimes she is then instructed to insert a tampon without removing its covering into the vaginal entrance and to leave it there for several hours, or until it feels entirely comfortable. The therapist can facilitate the process of deconditioning by warning the patient that she can expect to feel some unpleasant anxiety and tightness but *not* pain when she inserts an object into her vagina. But neither the anxiety nor the tightness will increase. To the contrary, if she can tolerate the feelings for a little while they will diminish and she will soon feel perfectly comfortable during penetration.

After the woman can comfortably tolerate insertion of her fingers and/or tampon the husband is included in the procedure. He is asked now to inspect his wife's vaginal entrance in full light. Then he repeats the procedure which she has carried out on herself previously. First he inserts his finger tip into her vaginal entrance. Then, while she is guiding and controlling his hand, he slips the whole finger into the vagina. Initially he holds it there quietly. Next he gently moves it in and out— does the same with two fingers. All this time the wife is assured that there will be *no* attempt made at penile penetration. If the husband becomes stimulated during vaginal play, the couple is instructed to engage in sexual activity which will provide him with an extravaginal orgasm.

The occasion of the first penile penetration is important. The couple agrees to this beforehand. The husband lubricates his erect penis and penetrates while she is guiding him. He quietly leaves his penis in the vagina for a few minutes without thrusting, then he withdraws. The couple may or may not choose extravaginal forms of sex play at this time.

After initial penetration, gentle thrusting and, next, thrusting to male, orgasm usually follows rapidly.

109

Reactions

For some women desensitization is a relatively easy procedure, while others become extremely anxious. The anxiety is mostly anticipatory, it is usually most marked just *prior* to and leading up to penile penetration. After penetration has occurred there is usually a dramatic abatement of anxiety.

The positive outcome of treatment by deconditioning the spastic vaginal response is virtually universal providing the couple completes the course of treatment. However, there are great variations in the results in terms of the couple's sexual functioning after penetration becomes possible. It comes as a surprise to many that vaginismic women are usually quite responsive and also easily orgastic on clitoral stimulation. Most women continue this good response after they are able to have intercourse. Some even become coitally orgastic rather rapidly. For these treatment can be terminated. In other cases successful treatment for vaginismus reveals other sexual problems in the woman and/or erectile and/or ejaculatory disorders in the husband. If such is the case further therapy is needed before the couple can enjoy good sexual functioning.

8

Impotence—Erectile Dysfunction

Erection is a neurovascular reflex which depends on a correct hormonal environment, a healthy penile anatomy, adequate vascular supply, and an intact and well-functioning nervous apparatus. Problems in any one of these components may cause potency disturbances on a physical basis. However, approximately 85 percent of impotence in the United States is strictly psychogenic. This is not surprising because even when there is physical integrity of the genital apparatus, the autonomic vascular reflexes which govern erection are delicate and subject to disruption by unconscious conflict and by emotion, i.e., anxiety and fear. Unless a man is in a calm emotional state and free of conflict while he is in the act of making love, his erectile reflexes are apt to be impaired.

In the past it was believed that psychogenic impotence is always the product of deeply neurotic conflict about sexuality. Specifically, according to psychoanalytic theory, unconscious fears of injury (castration) due to poorly resolved oedipal issues were the primary determinant of psychogenic impotence. More recently attention was focused on the dyadic (couple) causes of erectile difficulties and it was hypothesized that unconscious disturbance in the marital or love relationship, notably power struggles and contractual disappointments and mutual infantile transferences, were also capable of leading to erectile difficulties.

Clearly both unconscious and intrapsychic and dyadic conflicts can and do cause potency disorders. These conflicts are likely to emerge in the undefended man when he is about to engage in sexual activity. However many of the erectile disorders which we see in clinical practice are produced by simpler more easily correctible emotional factors. These include performance anxiety, fear of rejection by the woman, anticipation of impotence because of a past transient episode of erectile difficulty, overconcern with the woman's satisfaction, and culturally induced guilt about sexual enjoyment.

These concerns, as well as deeper fears, can intrude upon the man as he is making love and interfere with his abandonment to the sexual experience. Abandonment without interference by anxiety or by defenses against anxiety is a necessary condition for the smooth operation of the erectile reflexes.

Potency disorders which stem from such simpler antecedents are very often highly amenable to sex therapy, which always tries to humanize and demystify and diminish the anxiety which contaminates the sexual system between the partners. In this manner sexual abandonment becomes possible and potency is restored.

Treatment Strategy

The basic sequence employed in the brief active treatment of erectile dysfunction is as follows:

1. erotic pleasure without erection
2. erection without orgasm
3. extravaginal orgasm
4. intromission without orgasm
5. coitus

Each impotent patient's clinical situation must be individually evaluated in order to determine just what is causing the pathogenic anxiety and defenses at the moment of lovemaking. On the basis of these data, the sexual situation can be restructured to eliminate as many of the anxiety-provoking factors as possible. Some sex therapists do not structure the tasks on an individual basis, but routinely begin treatment with sensate focus I and II. There is a good rationale for such a pro-

Female stimulating male when he is partially clothed

cedure because these exercises are designed to eliminate much of the anxieties which operate in the average case. The prohibitions against having intercourse or orgasm eliminate performance anxiety, as does the therapist's suggestion that the reciprocal giving and receiving of pleasure be substituted for the goal of giving and eliciting a performance. Also "taking turns" eliminates the pressure created by making the man's response contingent upon his wife's. Usually a man will have spontaneous erections during sensate focus II. These may abate and return. This experience provides extremely important lessons for the couple, which should be made explicit by the therapist:

1. Under relaxed conditions erections will occur; i.e., the equipment is in good working order.

2. If an erection disappears it is not lost forever. It will come back in response to gentle stimulation. Indeed it is normal for erections to come and go during prolonged lovemaking, except at extremely young ages where they may persist for long periods of time.

SQUEEZE

Sometimes, in order to experientially confront an anxious man that he can regain a lost erection we use the "squeeze" technique which was originated by Masters and Johnson (see Figure 38). After a man has gained an erection the wife squeezes his penis just below the glans, with sufficient force that his erection abates. This does not usually hurt, but one third to one half of the erection abates, probably on a reflexive basis. Erections lost in this manner, return rapidly in response to gentle stimulation. Several repetitions of this maneuver generally suffice to cure a couple of the fear of losing the erection.

VARIATIONS IN STIMULATION

We also often start with sensate focus I and II but not invariably. Some men are actually inhibited by lengthy gentle foreplay. When the sexual evaluation reveals that there are some situations wherein the man is particularly potent we start with these. Thus for example some men who are troubled by erectile problems have excellent erections while they are "necking" with a woman while they are clothed. In such a case we might initiate treatment by having a man engage in love play while he keeps his clothes on. He is not allowed to have intercourse, but his wife stimulates his penis through his pants. At a later stage of treatment she may open his zipper and play with his penis, while he still keeps his pants on.

We also take advantage of the high morning androgen levels and the morning erection. It a man reports that he feels most aroused in the morning, and that he regularly wakes up with morning erections, we will prescribe sensate focus II in the early morning hours.

Sometimes we prescribe a lubricant, usually petroleum jelly. This substance is placed on the man's penis while his wife stimulates him, or while he stimulates himself in the presence of his wife. This is a most sensuous and arousing technique which seldom fails to produce an erection.

Oral stimulation is frequently used in this stage of treatment. For many men this is the most stimulating form of sexual activity and most likely to produce an erection. Naturally oral sex can be used only if the wife is willing and not repelled by the idea.

During stimulation whatever form this takes the man is admonished not to obsess, not to "spectator," i.e., watch if he is getting an erection or if he gets one to see "how hard it is."

If these techniques fail to protect him from anxiety, he is advised to immerse himself into a vivid erotic fantasy while he receives stimulation. Distraction from anxiety and from obsessive defenses against anxiety (self-observation or "spectatoring") by means of erotic fantasy has an important place in sex therapy. Erotic fantasies are ideal defenses against anxiety, while at the same time they facilitate the sexual response. The matter of fantasy must be handled with therapeutic sensitivity however. Couples often have intensely emotional reactions to their own and/or their mate's erotic fantasies. They are guilty and ashamed; they fear their content is "abnormal and sick"; they are jealous and/or guilty about the fact that someone or something else is

116

Couple stimulating each other—she is partially clothed (fantasy)

Female is stimulating male orally

being imagined during the sex act which is "supposed" to be just with each other.

If such emotional attitudes are mild and not deeply rooted in the couple's psychopathology, then an open discussion of each other's fantasies rapidly relieves guilt in each person and also promotes increased closeness between the couple and intimacy and erotic pleasure.

However, sometimes this is a difficult and delicate matter. An insecure spouse may actually experience a paranoid jealous reaction when she learns that her husband thinks of being fellated by a young stranger while he is making love to her. Such a response must be handled on a deeper level, one which transcends the narrow confines of a strictly symptom-oriented treatment. An adverse response to fantasy leads into important work with the patient's insecure self-esteem, into the fundamentally poor regard for herself, which is the root from which her lack of acceptance of her partner's normal erotic fantasy life grows.

Reactions

This regimen of intense erotic stimulation together with the relief of the necessity to perform frequently produces erection within a few days. Some men get irritable because they are not "allowed" to ejaculate during this period of time, but this does not pose any significant obstacle to therapy. There are some men, however, who fail to respond to these procedures. In such cases psychodynamic exploration of the anxieties and conflicts and marital difficulties may be attempted. However, in such cases the impotence is probably directly related to deep-seated intrapsychic and/or marital pathology and such patients are not usually amenable to brief treatment procedures. If a man fails to respond to behavioral prescriptions designed to produce erection without orgasm, his prognosis with sex therapy is poor.

Extravaginal Orgasm

After the man has gained confidence that he can have an erection, therapy proceeds to orgasm produced by manual and/or oral stimulation. The procedure is exactly as before except that he may ejaculate if he chooses to.

Some wives of impotent men are unable or unwilling to climax on clitoral stimulation and demand intercourse as their sole means of satisfaction. This demand places the man under great stress as he must perform with an erection or his wife remains unsatisfied. In such cases we shift the focus of therapy to the wife. We attempt to get her to accept extracoital orgasm as an alternative form of satisfaction. This may entail considerable psychotherapeutic work. But this is an extremely important aspect of therapy which usually does much to relieve the man's sense of pressure and need to "perform." He can now give pleasure to his wife with his hands or his mouth over which he has voluntary control. She is no longer dependent on an erect penis over which there is no voluntary control. She will no longer feel rejected if he does not erect—and he in turn will no longer fear rejection by her if he can caress her to orgasm and does not have to produce an erection to "prove" that he loves her or that he is a "real man."

Intromission Without Orgasm

Before actual coitus to orgasm it is often advisable to "practice" vaginal containment. The couple is instructed to engage in the same sort of erotic play which has produced erection during the previous week. When erection is secure, the man enters the woman for a little while. He may thrust a few times, but he may not ejaculate inside the vagina. Orgasm occurs extravaginally as before, after he has withdrawn. In some cases intromission should be under the control of the man, i.e., he enters and pulls out when he is moved to. In other cases, it is less anxiety producing and more stimulating for the man if his wife is in "charge" of his penis. In the female superior position she plays with his penis until he obtains a good erection. Then she guides his penis into her vagina. She thrusts a few times and withdraws the penis and plays with it again. This procedure may be repeated several times. Again ejaculation at this phase of therapy should be extravaginal.

Female is stimulating male manually with petroleum jelly

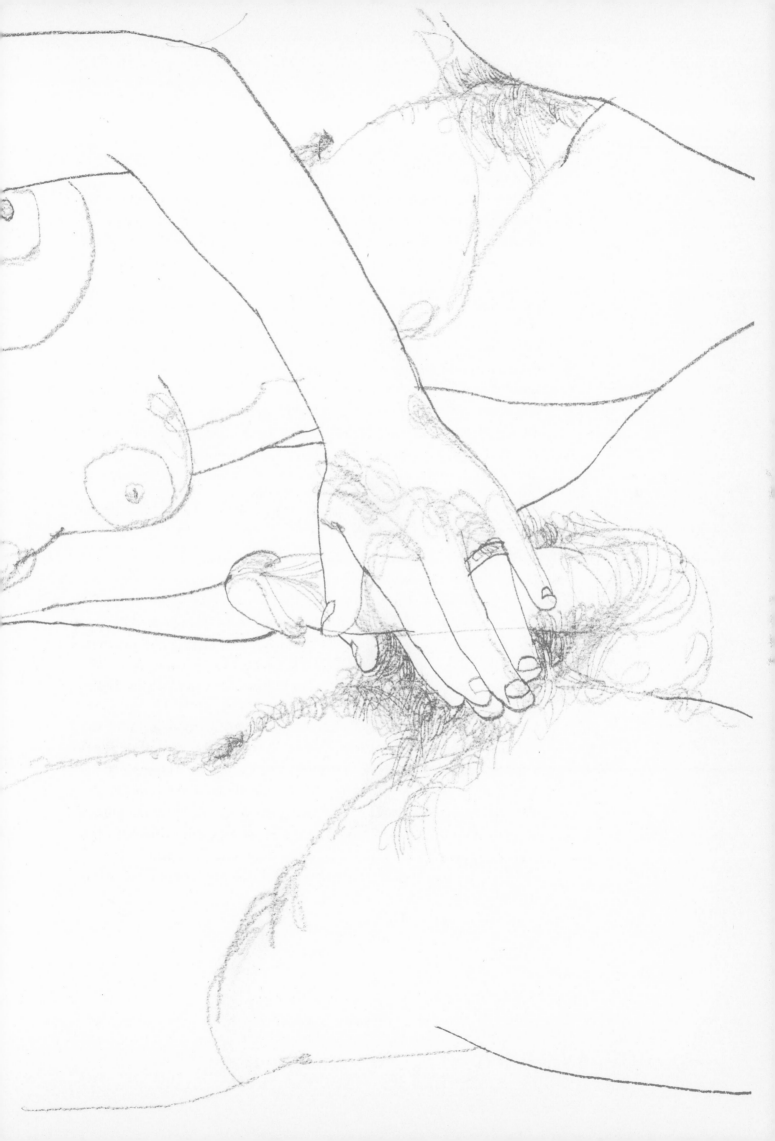

Female superior—female stimulating male's erect penis

Coitus

The initial coital experience may produce some anxiety and therefore should be structured so that it is as reassuring and stimulating as possible.

The man is usually given an "out." He is advised to engage in the same sort of sex play described in the previous section on "intromission without orgasm." He is told he now may ejaculate intravaginally if he is moved to. However if he is not moved to, if he has any doubts about his ability to function, he must withdraw and have his orgasm outside the vagina, or, in other cases, have no orgasm at all.

He is advised, in the presence of his wife whose feelings are of vital importance in this matter, to be "selfish." In order to function he must allow himself to abandon himself to his emotions and sensations to the exclusion of concern for his partner, *for that moment.* His "selfishness" is temporary, for if she is not satisfied by his spontaneous excitement and surge towards orgasm, he can satisfy her with a clitorally induced orgasm after he has ejaculated.

He is advised to employ fantasy, as well as any pace no matter how rapid, or any position or technique which is most reassuring and exciting to him. All these devices are temporary and tend to fall into disuse when coital security is reestablished. However, if in the future the man has some transient anxiety which again impairs his erectile response, he can avail himself of the techniques he has learned during sex therapy to help himself over his difficulties.

Reactions

The rapid relief of impotence, or for that matter the rapid relief of any sexual dysfunction, usually evokes relief and pleasure in the symptomatic patient. However, occasionally when the symptoms have served an unconscious defensive purpose, there is some anxiety or depression as sexual functioning is restored. It should be noted however that the partner may have an even more intense emotional response to her husband's sudden new potency. She may also have mixed reactions.

127

Some women are unambivalently happy at their husband's improvement and show this positive motivation in speech and in deed. Others, however, are threatened. These may verbalize their anxiety, or it may show in an unexplained depressed or anxious mood. Still others act out their conflict and unconsciously place obstacles in the path of their husband's treatment.

Sabotage of treatment and of a mate's sexual functioning can take many subtle forms. It can be as fleeting as a loss of interest, a lack of warmth and encouragement, a subtle critical attitude toward the husband. These attitudes usually become apparent during the therapeutic sessions. The wife's attitude may simply change from one of support to increasing detachment or demand. Or the wife's resistance may be blatantly obvious. She may become anxious or depressed, start drinking heavily, and/or complain that the exercises are tedious, boring, and mechanical. She may become openly critical, go on a spending spree. In one of my cases the wife started an extramarital affair just at the point where her husband began to get good erections.

The sources of negative partner reaction to rapid sexual improvement in the spouse are often unconscious hostility towards him and even more commonly the unconscious fear of losing him now that he is potent and virile. Some persons have psychological investments in their lover's inadequacy. Such women harbor deep feelings of insecurity. Unconsciously they believe, "I am not very attractive. He only stays with me because he is dependent on me for I tolerate his impotence. Now that he can function he will leave me and find a more adequate and attractive woman." The result of such an unconscious fear may be the sabotage of therapy in subtle or obvious ways. Sex therapy is not completed until such painful and sensitive issues have been adequately resolved and the partner is reassured. In the face of an unhappy and threatened spouse, one cannot expect a "cure" of the potency disorder to remain stable. There is a high probability of relapse unless both sexual partners' problems are resolved at least to the point of emotional stability.

Female superior—inserting his penis into her vagina

9

Retarded Ejaculation — Ejaculatory Overcontrol

Retarded ejaculation is an involuntary inhibition of the male orgastic reflex. This condition is physiologically analogous to female orgasmic dysfunction. The retarded ejaculator is able to feel sexual excitement and have good erections, but even though he receives what should be ample stimulation, he has difficulty releasing this ejaculatory reflex. Severe overcontrol, i.e., the man who has never ejaculated at all, even on masturbation, is rare. This is fortunate because this extreme form of retardation is difficult to treat. In its milder forms ejaculatory retardation (or ejaculatory incompetence) is relatively common and has an excellent prognosis with sex therapy. In the moderate forms of this disorder the man can only ejaculate on masturbation when he is alone. Men suffering from milder retardation can climax in the presence of their partner but only in response to manual and/or oral stimulation. They cannot ejaculate in the vagina. Still milder forms are situational and some merely require excessively long and vigorous coitus in order to ejaculate.

The pathogenesis of ejaculatory overcontrol is similar to that of constipation, globus hystericus, and difficulty with starting the stream of urine. Defecation, swallowing, urination, and ejaculation or orgasm all depend on autonomically mediated reflexes which are normally brought under voluntary control. When the individual is in an emotionally aroused state or when he is under the domination of a psychological conflict, there may be an involuntary defensive reaction of inhibition of the reflex in question. The defensive reaction entails an overcontrol, i.e., the inability to release the reflex from cortical control.

The source of the unconscious conflict and/or the content of the emotional state seems to be nonspecific. In other words it has not been possible to identify a specific psychodynamic constellation which would discriminate ejaculatory incompetence from impotence. The same kinds of deeply unconscious castration fears and superficial performance anxieties, as well as fears about commitment to the partner will result in erectile difficulties in one man and ejaculatory overcontrol in another. The conflicts seem the same, but the *defenses* are distinct. The retarded ejaculator will unconsciously "hold back," i.e., exercise control and so avoid anxiety, while the impotent man allows himself to be flooded with anxiety which then ruins his erectile response.

The main purpose of brief, active sex therapy with retarded ejaculation is to *distract* the man from his excessive need to control, so that his orgastic reflexes can discharge unimpeded. Often this strategy works very well. At other times some of the underlying conflicts must be recognized and resolved, at least in part, before the patient can relax enough to allow himself to be so distracted. For these patients a very important factor involved in the anxiety and inhibitory defense against this anxiety is the relationship with the partner. Considerable resolution of unconscious problems in the relationship usually needs to be accomplished before the patient can relax and have easy and pleasurable orgasms.

Treatment Strategy

Two basic treatment principles govern the therapy of retarded ejaculation:*

1. progressive in-vivo desensitization to intravaginal ejaculation (i.e., desensitization in the presence of the partner);
2. stimulation with concomitant distraction.

PROGRESSIVE DESENSITIZATION

Most retarded ejaculators can ejaculate under some condition and the basic strategy of treatment is to gradually shape the patient's ejac-

* The treatment rationale of retarded ejaculation of men and orgastic dysfunction of women is analogous.

ulatory response toward the desired goal of ejaculatory freedom on coitus. Techniques are structured with this principle in mind. Therefore, the specific behavioral prescriptions will vary with the individual case.

For example, a patient can ejaculate only if his wife has left the house and he is alone. If he then masturbates with petroleum jelly to a fantasy of being orally stimulated by a strange woman, he can predictably reach orgasm. When he tries to make love to his wife, he has pleasure, a good erection, intercourse, she is satisfied, but he does not reach orgasm no matter if coitus lasts for one hour. His erection slowly abates and he goes to sleep.

This material is openly discussed with both partners. The first behavioral prescription in this case might be that he masturbate in his usual fashion with his usual fantasy behind locked doors while his wife is downstairs. If this is successful, several days later he might repeat the procedure while his wife is in the adjacent room. Next, while she is in the same room. Later on, they make love and after she is satisfied, he goes to the bathroom to masturbate to orgasm. This sequence begins to establish an association between the heterosexual act and orgasm. A key point in treatment occurs when the patient's wife can manually stimulate him to orgasm. She uses the petroleum jelly and he is advised to use his fantasy while he is being stimulated. These may be covert or openly talked about with his wife during the sexual act. [This use of fantasy is an expression of the second principle of treatment: *distraction* from excessive control and self-observation during stimulation.]

After the patient has been brought to orgasm by his wife, further lone masturbatory release is prohibited. He can only now ejaculate in the presence of and with the participation of his wife. Ejaculation progressively nearer the vagina is the next sequence of treatment.

The *male bridge maneuver* is employed after the patient can reliably have orgasm with her manual manipulation. The woman stimulates the man with the petroleum jelly until he is near orgasm. Then he enters. She stimulates his penis with her hand while he thrusts. Figures 32 and 33 illustrate two coital positions wherein this technique is comfortable and feasible.

After the man has penetrated the vagina with a combination of hand

133

Male masturbating—female's back is turned

Male masturbating—female in his arms

Female stimulating male—his hand is on hers

Female stimulating male's penis near her vaginal entrance

and vaginal stimulation, he begins to signal when he is at the point of orgasm so that she can withdraw her hand and let the coital thrusting bring about the actual orgasm. A position wherein the woman keeps her legs tightly closed during coitus (see Figure 34) increases penile friction and is sometimes useful at this stage of treatment.

STIMULATION AND DISTRACTION

The crucial principle which governs the treatment both of retarded ejaculation of the male and orgastic inhibition of the female is that the person be physically stimulated intensely, while at the same time mentally distracted from inhibitory vigilance. It has already been mentioned that mental absorption in erotic fantasy while genital stimulation is being experienced, is an ideal method of releasing the orgasm reflex. However, some patients require more complete or concrete distraction, because they are unable to lose themselves in their imageries and fantasies. In such cases I might advise that the patient read erotic literature or view sexually stimulating pictures while stimulation occurs. Thus for example, one woman has her first orgasm when reading an erotic novel while she stimulated herself with a vibrator.

Incompletely Retarded Ejaculation

There is a rare syndrome which conceptually belongs under the category of retarded ejaculation—which I have called *incompletely or partially retarded ejaculation*. In this syndrome only one phase, the ejaculatory component of the orgasm response, is inhibited, while the other component of the male orgasm, emission, is not impaired. The male orgasm consists of first, *emission*, which is a sympathetically mediated contraction of the vas deferens, prostate, and seminal vesicles. This gathers the ejaculate into the posterior urethra. This response is perceived without pleasure as the "sensation of ejaculatory inevitability." The ejaculatory component of this male orgasm normally follows a fraction of a second later. It consists of rhythmic contractions of

143

the striated muscles at the base of the penis. This part of the response is associated with the intense pleasure of orgasm and this produces the squirting action of ejaculation.

The man who suffers from incomplete retardation has good and pleasurable erections. But at the point of climax he only experiences the emission phase of the response. Perceptually he feels a "release" but *no* orgasmic pleasure. Physiologically there is only a seepage of semen and also a very slow detumescence (because the vasocongestion is not "pumped out" by the muscle contractions).

This extremely rare syndrome is sometimes confused with retrograde ejaculation which is quite different. In retrograde ejaculation the ejaculate empties into the bladder because the internal vesicular sphincter is paralyzed by anticholinergic drugs or by disease. The muscles at the base of the penis contract normally and orgasm is pleasurable in all respects but it is "dry," i.e., there is no external ejaculate.

The few patients with partial retardation whom I have treated have all had trouble abandoning themselves to the sexual experience. They tended to be overcontrolled, overly-self-critical, and performance oriented. These defenses were evoked by a variety of unconscious insecurities and conflicts. Treatment follows one of the same principles as retarded ejaculation: stimulation with concomitant relaxation and distraction.

One of my patients had his first complete and pleasurable orgasm when he was being stimulated by his partner while he was absorbed in watching an erotic film.

Another guide to the treatment of retarded ejaculation is to increase stimulation by structuring the tasks so that ejaculatory urgency builds up, while at the same time the obsessive defense of overcontrol is diminished. Patients who suffer from partial and total retardation tend to report that as pleasurable sexual tension builds up and they reach a stage premonitory to orgasm, they wonder "Will it be a good orgasm this time?" or "Will I have an orgasm soon?" If the patient experiences this, he is advised that he is *not* to ejaculate on that occasion. He is to withdraw his penis and desist from further stimulation. If it happens the next time he tries sex the admonition is repeated. He is only allowed to ejaculate if he does not stop to think about the process.

144

Position for female touching male's penis during coitus—male superior

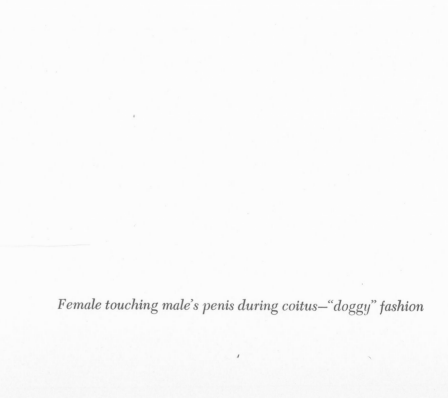

Female touching male's penis during coitus—"doggy" fashion

Coitus with female's legs tightly closed

Reactions

Again there is no data to justify the conclusion of specificity in sexual dysfunction. In other words we can not say that impotence is specifically caused by unconscious castration anxiety or by performance anxiety. *Any* source of anxiety is capable of impairing the erectile reflex. And while castration and performance anxieties are frequently encountered in this population, they are by no means the universal causes. Similarly conflicts of any sort and defenses against these can produce inhibition of the orgastic reflex. However two conflicts do emerge with predictable frequency when treating the *retarded ejaculator,* namely: fear of involvement with the woman, and related conflicts centering around hostility and sadistic impulses toward women. During the course of treatment with these couples it is often revealed that the man is really "holding back" psychologically as well as physiologically with his orgasm. Frequently also a great deal of hostility to women is evident of which man is unaware. The patient must often be confronted with this hostility. And more important its sources must often be explored and resolved before he can enjoy orgastic freedom. Most such patients are extremely guilty about their aggressive impulses and therefore defend themselves against these in elaborate and tenacious ways. Resolution of guilt through reassurance that these impulses are not evil, that when people are angry there is a good reason, that anger is basically a constructive and adaptive impulse, are all important parts of the treatment strategy with this patient population.

151

10

Premature Ejaculation– Inadequate Ejaculatory Control

Premature ejaculation is the favorite dysfunction of sex therapists because although it is highly prevalent and troublesome, it is extremely easy to treat with sex therapy in most cases. Yet it is resistant to other forms of treatment.

The prematurely ejaculating patient reaches climax so rapidly that lovemaking is often disappointing for both partners. The essence of prematurity is lack of adequate voluntary control over the ejaculatory reflex. Some reflexes are subject to voluntary control and others are not. Erection in men and genital vasocongestion in women cannot be brought under voluntary control. Ejaculation and orgasm can. The normal person can delay orgasm and "let it go" when it is desired. The premature ejaculator cannot. He ejaculates reflexively as soon as he reaches a critical level of excitement.

I have hypothesized that the reason that the premature ejaculator has not learned ejaculatory continence is that he is not *aware* of the sensations that are premonitory to orgasm. That is probably because he experiences some anxiety at this time which distracts him. Conscious perception of the sensations leading to a reflex, as for example urination or defecation, are prerequisite for learning voluntary control.

152

Treatment Strategy

Successful treatment consists of fostering the patient's clear perception of the sensations premonitory to orgasm. This should be done under tranquil conditions, in the presence of and with the participation of his wife.

There are two methods which have proven successful in the treatment of premature ejaculation and they both seem to be governed by the same mechanism of action, namely fostering pre-ejaculatory awareness in the heterosexual situation. The first is the "squeeze" method of Masters and Johnson and the second is the "stop—start" technique. This technique was invented by James Semans and has been adapted for use in sex therapy by me at the Cornell Clinic.

STOP—START

Initially the patient practices control while he is being manually stimulated by his wife.

The couple is instructed to make love in their usual fashion until he has a good erection. Then he lies on his back, closes his eyes, and his wife masturbates him. He is told to keep his attention focused sharply on his erotic sensation. When he feels near orgasm he tells his wife to stop. In a few seconds the ejaculatory urge will abate and he then tells her to start stimulating him again. Again he stops short of ejaculation. This is repeated four times. On the fourth trial he ejaculates. The patient is admonished *not* to let anything distract him. In contrast to impotence and retarded ejaculation where *distraction* with fantasy is emphasized, in premature ejaculation the patient must *desist* from distracting himself. The essence of the treatment is that he stay closely with his experience of mounting excitement and learn to recognize the signs of impending orgasm.

After two successful trials the couple repeats the same procedure, this time using petroleum jelly as a lubricant. This is very arousing and closely simulates the vaginal environment.

Three or four successful trials with lubricant and the couple is ready

Stop–Start—Female is stimulating man's penis manually

Stop–Start—Female superior—coital position

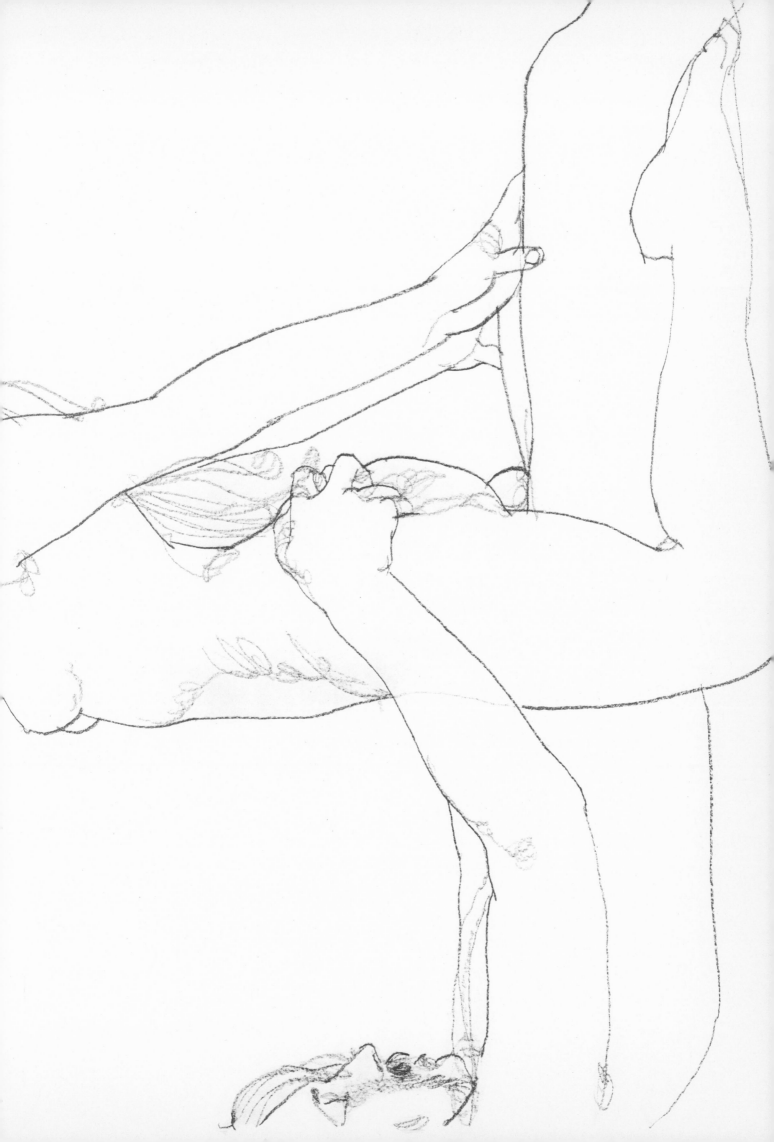

for coitus. This is also done within the stop–start format. The woman assumes the female superior position. The penis is inserted and he places his hands on her hips and guides her up and down until he is near orgasm. Then he stops her. A few seconds later, after the ejaculatory urge is gone, they resume. He does not thrust initially. On the fourth time he thrusts and comes. Again it is exceedingly important that he keep his attention focused on his sensations during this exercise. Three or four female superior stop–start exercises, with him thrusting more and more as they go on, and the couple is ready to do the same in the side-to-side position. The male superior is the most difficult from the standpoint of ejaculatory control and is done last.

Usually a man gains a good deal of ejaculatory control in from 2 to 10 weeks. Perfect control however is not usually attained until several months after termination of treatment. During this time the couple is advised to do one "stop–start" exercise per week.

SQUEEZE

The "squeeze" method advocated by Masters and Johnson contains essentially the same ingredients as the "stop–start" method described herein. The only difference is that instead of *stopping* the woman *squeezes* her husband's penis. Specifically she grasps the erect penis between forefingers and thumb just below the glans and presses hard until he loses a good part of his erection. Then she resumes stimulation.*

During the female superior coital exercises the squeeze technique is also employed. Here the woman removes the penis from her vagina and squeezes it until the erection abates. Then she stimulates him, and when the erection returns, she mounts him and resumes thrusting.

REACTIONS

1. *Boredom.* If the training period lasts more than a few weeks the routine is apt to get tedious for the couple. For this reason it is my

---

* Dr. Alex Levai who has been trained by Masters and Johnson has informed me that they are currently advocating that the female squeeze the man's penis, not on his request, but on a random basis.

practice to allow one "free," i.e., spontaneous, no stop–start lovemaking session during the week, after 3 weeks or so.

2. *Frustration by the woman.* She may become aroused and frustrated during the training period. For this reason, and if she desires it, the couple is encouraged to engage in sex play which provides her with orgasm through clitoral stimulation. This must never be at the cost of distracting the man from concentrating on his stop–start exercises. He must put all thoughts of his wife out of mind while he is being stimulated, or the exercise will not be successful. For these reasons clitoral stimulation for her occurs after the man has ejaculated. Both in the extravaginal and stop–start coital phases of the treatment program.

3. *Resistances.* The two phases of therapy, i.e., extravaginal and coital stimulation, tend to elicit different kinds of emotional responses from couples. Again, both provide a therapeutic challenge because they present obstacles to the progress of treatment. They also are a unique opportunity for significant therapeutic intervention in the couple's and each partner's deeper conflicts.

If the wife is hostile toward her husband she may react with anger at being used as a "Geisha girl" in the first phase of treatment when she is stimulating his penis. By contrast when the couple has an unambivalently loving relationship, the wife finds her help-agent role immensely satisfying, and she takes pleasure in her husband's progress.

The manual stop–start exercises have the potential for also evoking profound feelings and defenses against these feelings in the man himself. A man who is basically insecure about his worth and his essential "lovableness" often erects defenses of overconcern with his partner and compulsive attention to her needs. The stop–start exercise deactivates this defense. He is forced into the previously avoided position of having to receive and to accept stimulation from his partner. This change can give rise to considerable anxiety in some patients. Sometimes the anxiety manifests as fear of being rejected by the wife. More seriously troubled men will occasionally respond to this situation with paranoid defenses. Some are emotionally unable to go through the exercises without prior resolution of their basic insecurities by means of psychotherapy.

There are also some positive emotional reactions to stop–start. Often it enables men to enjoy the passive role in sexual relations for the first

162

Squeeze

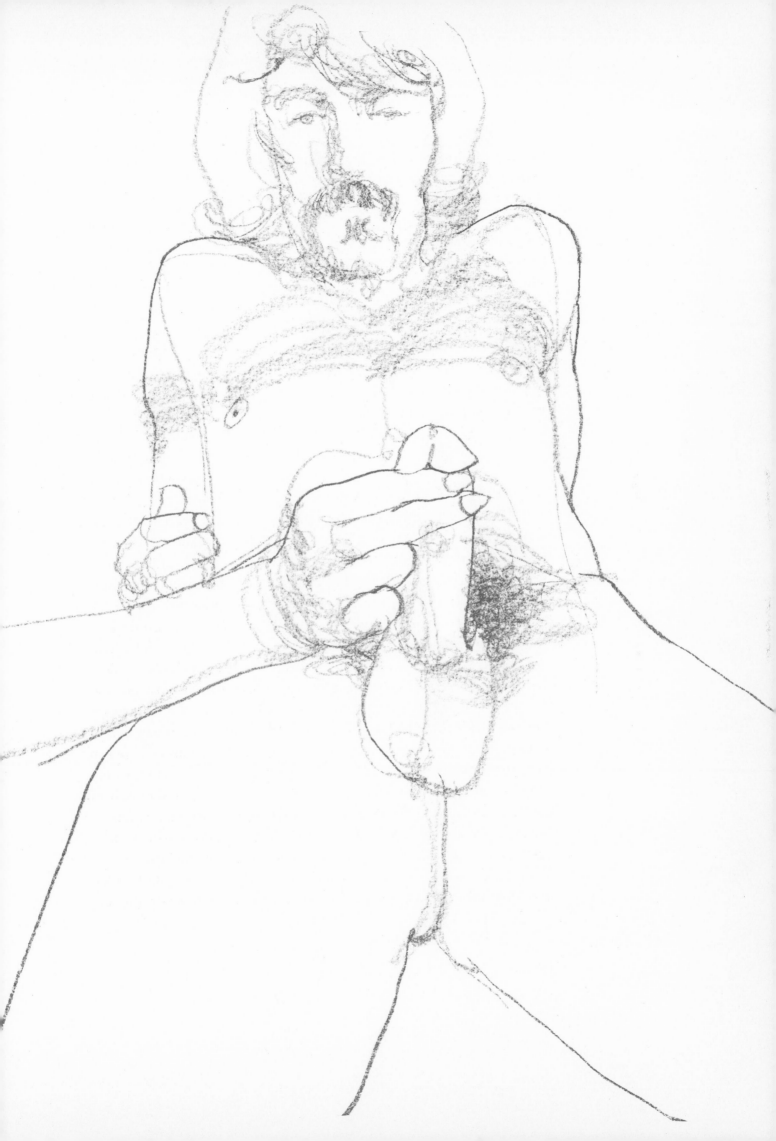

time. They learn it is pleasurable to receive as well as to give. He learns that his wife loves him and will not reject him even though she is delaying her gratification for him and giving to him, and he is not "serving" her.

While the extragenital phase of treatment is apt to elicit emotional reactions related to giving and taking and the husband's passive-receptive role, the coital stop–start exercises typically elicit emotional responses which are evoked by the man's rapid improvement. By the time treatment has progressed to the female-superior stop–start, the man has gained a considerable amount of ejaculatory control. In uncomplicated cases this improved functioning elicits joy and relief in both spouses. However, improvement may also be very threatening to both. The woman, especially, is apt to become depressed or anxious at this time. She may be in touch with these feelings and their sources and experience them as such, or she may be unaware and act these out by sabotaging treatment. This can be done by refusing to cooperate, by communicating her boredom with the exercises or, worse, her growing loathing for them. Some women attack their husbands at this point. They criticize and discourage them, letting them know that even though they may gain ejaculatory control they remain inadequate and repulsive in other areas.

Such adverse emotional responses to a husband's improvement are most often rooted in the wife's deep insecurities. She feels inadequate and insecure and unable to hold on to her man. His disability and her tolerance of it made him dependent on her. Now that he is about to be functional, will he not seek out other, more attractive women? Clearly, reassurance that she is valued and loved for her own sake is therapeutically indicated at this time.

Another source of anxiety, now that the husband can function, involves the wife's own sexual adequacy. Many wives of premature ejaculators suffer from some measure of orgastic dysfunction. Not surprisingly they and their husbands attribute this to his difficulty. After all, how could a woman be expected to respond with orgasm when the man ejaculates so rapidly. However, this assumption is false in a large proportion of cases where the wife has an independent sexual dysfunction of her own. Her husband's ejaculatory problem has long

165

served to obscure her problem, and the fact that he can now have intercourse for quite a long period of time and she does not climax confronts the couple with her problem. This can be quite threatening. Especially if it has been the family saga to consider him the problem and her the martyr.

To forestall such reactions I always make it quite clear during the initial session that premature ejaculation has a good prognosis. We will first treat the husband's premature ejaculation. But successful ejaculatory control on his part does *not* guarantee the wife's good functioning. It specifically does not. The woman's sexual functioning can only be assessed *after* he has gained control. If there turns out to be a problem, this will be treated at that time.

While the discovery of an orgastic problem in the spouse of a previously premature ejaculator occasions some adverse reactions, the ultimate outcome is good because it provides an opportunity for the wife to derive the benefit of treatment as well. However, such adverse reactions of a wife to a husband's improvement must be handled with therapeutic sensitivity or they can motivate the premature termination of therapy, before the man has gained ejaculatory continence.

On rare occasions, the symptomatic man may also be threatened by his own improvement. The symptom may serve an unconscious need, if, for example, it is his only "hold out" to a dominating mother-figure wife. Then treatment may reach an impasse at the point of coitus, or the man may become impotent. In such cases unconscious conflict must be resolved in order for the symptom to improve. In my experience the rare premature ejaculator who is not helped by the treatment procedure outlined above is likely to be troubled with unconscious resistance of this sort. Perhaps there is a small subgroup of premature ejaculators who are not amenable to a training procedure designed to provide sensory feedback of ejaculatory sensations. However, present evidence suggests that all premature ejaculators can respond to these measures except for those wherein ejaculatory incontinence serves a deep psychological need which cannot be bypassed by behavioral means.

166

III
CONCLUSIONS

11

The Role of Psychodynamics
in Sex Therapy

As I review this manual of sex therapy I am uneasy because too much stress seems to have been placed on the sexual mechanics. It was the prime objective of the book to provide a clear description of the most frequently used exercises and when possible to conceptualize their underlying rationale. But in addition, I have also tried to stress the importance of the emotional reactions which patients have to these tasks.

Despite my efforts in this respect, the approach still seems too mechanical. I hope I have managed to place sufficient emphasis on the importance of integrating the tasks with psychotherapy. I hope there has been enough stress on the challenges and opportunities for dealing with deeper psychic issues provided by the emotional reactions of patients to these exercises. The beauty of this method of sex therapy lies in combining structured sexual interactions with psychotherapy. In actual practice *most* of the therapist's activities are psychotherapeutic and consist of active interpretation, support, clarification, and integration of the experiences with the couple in the office sessions. This dynamic interplay between experience and psychotherapy constitutes the essence of the new sex therapy. Often psychotherapy centers around the couples' resistances to the therapeutic exercises.

Resistances to Sex Therapy

It was Freud who formulated the concept of resistance. He observed that his patients resisted getting well in psychoanalysis. He explained this surprising phenomena as being caused by the patients' unconscious attempts to defend against conscious recognition of their anxiety-provoking unconscious conflicts. In order to avoid conscious recognition of unconscious conflict they attempted to sabotage analysis. But the concept of resistance has wider application. It pertains to anxiety generated by facing one's problems, giving up defenses, and changing one's behavior. Thus patients unconsciously resist sex therapy very much the same way that they resist psychoanalysis, and unless he is prepared for this, the novice therapist will be surprised and troubled when his patients fail to perform the prescribed tasks and come to the therapeutic sessions with obvious rationalizations.

A distinction must be drawn between resistance to the *process* and to the *outcome* of sex therapy. As has been repeatedly stressed, patients may have intense negative emotional responses to engaging in the prescribed exercises and erotic interactions of sex therapy. Other patients and their spouses are resistant to the outcome of sex therapy; i.e., good sexual functioning mobilizes anxiety and guilt.

RESISTANCE TO THE OUTCOME OF SEX THERAPY

Many persons are made anxious by success and pleasure. Fat persons are afraid to become thin, poor people are afraid to make money, and sexually dysfunctional persons are sometimes covertly afraid to achieve the sexual fulfillment which they so ardently desire on a conscious level. The unconscious roots of the fear of success vary. Sometimes anticipation of injury born of unresolved incestuous taboos play a role. Sometimes unconscious fears of loss of love and abandonment play a role. But whatever the unconscious roots may be, the anticipation or achievement of sexual success arouses a negative emotional response in some persons and so mobilizes resistance to the treatment.

Improvement of sexual functioning in a *mate* may also be deeply threatening because an insecure person may fear that a sexually adequate partner will abandon them. Again such feelings of threat may cause the mate to resist, i.e., to place various obstacles in the way of therapy.

Actually the dangers of a patient's sustaining emotional trauma as a result of successful outcome of sex therapy have been exaggerated by psychoanalytically oriented writers. Psychoanalytic theory predicts that *all* symptomatic improvement, unless it is the product of conflict resolution on an unconscious level, will be accompanied by significant anxiety and/or the development of substitute symptoms. These patients now express the same conflicts and/or guard against the same psychic "dangers" which were formerly the function of the sexual symptom. There are theoretic fallacies in this reasoning which are beyond this discussion. But from a practical perspective clinical evidence indicates that only a small segment of the patient population responds with significant anxiety to improved sexual functioning as predicted by analytic theory. However, *transient* improvement anxiety is very common and the therapist must remain alert for the possibility that the symptomatic patient and/or his spouse will resist getting sexually well because of such neurotic anxiety and guilt. Actually such transient improvement anxiety is not detrimental to therapy. In fact it provides an excellent opportunity for psychodynamic clarification and resolution of the patient's deeper underlying conflicts.

Learning theory predicts the opposite consequences of successful therapy. According to this frame of reference the patient will react purely positively when his symptom is removed. In fact his improvement will generalize and he will function better in other spheres of behavior as well. Accordingly there is no unconscious resistance to treatment. In actual fact *some* patients *do* respond as predicted by the behaviorists. Some patients and their spouses evidence undiluted joy at their improved sexual functioning and enjoy the process of therapy without ambivalence. But these patients are definitely in the minority.

Clinical observation of couples who undergo sex therapy reveals that the great majority show some degree, albeit mild, of adverse emotional reactions to a favorable outcome of therapy. For the healthier couples these tend to be transient and largely anticipatory. Once sexual functioning is established most patients feel wonderful and their relationships improve as well. Sicker patients are more likely to respond to a favorable outcome with a more serious or mixed or negative response. Once again skillful and sensitive psychotherapeutic management of improvement anxiety is crucial for favorable outcome in treatment with a major segment of the sex therapy population.

RESISTANCE TO THE PROCESS OF SEX THERAPY

Not only the outcome, but also the very *process* of sex therapy may mobilize resistance. The sexual techniques often force persons to experience behavior which they have previously avoided because this would mobilize anxiety, anger, or guilt. The techniques entail touching gently, kissing, displaying sensitivity to a partner's needs and wishes, and expressing tenderness—forms of behavior which promote involvement and intimacy and openness. This may be extremely threatening to a person who defends himself from hurt with distance, alienation, and control of his emotions. It is not surprising that patients will resist therapy when this occurs. They may admit their uneasiness to themselves, their spouses, and the therapist. More commonly, conscious awareness of these dynamics is too threatening. Instead they "act out." They avoid the tasks or do them in a clumsy or hostile or mechanical manner. They rationalize. They quarrel with their mates. They attack the therapist and/or the therapy, and so on. The therapist must remain alert to such resistance. Clarification and resolution or bypass is essential if therapy is to succeed.

This *process* of sex therapy not only may cause difficulty in either partner individually but it also frequently threatens the balance of the *marital dyad*. Sex therapy makes an effort to change the dyadic system which exists between the spouses. The sexual interactions of the couple must be changed in the course of treatment from alienating to human, from uncommunicative and secretive to open and authentic, from hostile to loving. Especially when each feels insecure with the other, changing interactional patterns may be temporarily painful. The pain may last until security is reestablished on a more realistic basis. The process of disrupting established interactions entailed in sex therapy can be very threatening and so mobilize resistance in either or both partners.

172

Prognosis in Sex Therapy

The outcome of sex therapy depends on three factors: the nature of the dysfunction, the structure and depth of the intrapsychic pathology of each partner, and the quality of the marital relationship.

The dysfunctions have different prognoses with sex therapy. *Premature ejaculation, vaginismus,* and the *total anorgasticity of women* all have excellent outcomes with sex therapy.

It is very seldom that a *premature ejaculator* doesn't learn good ejaculatory control within a few weeks to months. This condition seems to be relatively independent of intrapsychic and marital pathology and tends to improve even when it occurs in highly neurotic men whose marriages are troubled. As long as the relationship is stable enough for therapeutic cooperation, and as long as a man can concentrate on his premonitory sensations while he is being stimulated by his wife, in our experience, he will learn ejaculatory continence.*

The same can essentially be said for *vaginismus.* As long as the patient can be induced to tolerate progressively larger objects in her vagina she will be "cured" rapidly. The deconditioning seems to be relatively independent of any concomitant psycho- and marital pathology which may exist. However, mere deconditioning of a spastic vaginal introitus does not insure good and pleasurable sexual functioning. And indeed, after the vagina is open for coitus the couple's sexual adjustment varies greatly. Some couples function well and need no further treatment when penetration becomes possible. For other couples the newfound ability to have intercourse reveals orgastic or response problems in the wife and/or potency and ejaculatory problems in the husband. These then require further therapeutic intervention.

The woman who has never had an orgasm also has an excellent prognosis for learning to climax with sex therapy. Actually this is surprising because, in contrast with premature ejaculation and vaginismus, the other two dysfunctions which have excellent prognoses and which are relatively dissociated from psychodynamics, female orgasm is closely related to unconscious and dynamic psychic factors. Nevertheless, on

---

* There may exist a small subgroup of premature ejaculators whose disorder is the product of a different pathogenesis. These may account for the few failures which are reported.

173

an empirical basis, it is extremely unusual to fail to be able to teach a woman to reach orgasm in a brief period of time. However the ultimate outcome of treatment with this population varies greatly. Some women learn to masturbate to orgasm but go no further than this. Others progress to partner-related orgastic experiences and some become coitally orgastic.

Treatment of *erectile* and *situational orgastic dysfunctions* is more complex, and outcome is more variable. This is probably because these syndromes are intimately enmeshed in the psychic matrix in which they occur.

The *erectile dysfunctions* have a moderately good prognosis with sex therapy. Potency seems to be more directly related to a man's psychic and emotional state than does ejaculatory control. When emotional disturbances can be easily corrected or bypassed prognosis with sex therapy is excellent. When the negative emotional responses to sexual intercourse with a woman have deep and tenacious roots, prognosis is more guarded. In actual clinical practice the majority of secondary potency disorders have a favorable outcome. Sex therapy is highly effective in humanizing the sexual situation and reducing those superficial sources of sexually destructive tensions and anxieties which are so prevalent in our culture. However, sex therapy is only moderately successful (approximately 50 percent) in the primary erectile dysfunctions and also is of limited effectiveness in those dysfunctions which are clearly and directly related to profound psychopathology and marital disharmony. However, even neurotic patients should be given the benefits of a trial of brief, active sex therapy, because by using psychodynamic methods it is often possible to bypass even formidable psychopathology and get the patient to function sexually regardless.

Situational orgastic dysfunction has a mixed prognosis with sex therapy. In the course of treatment almost all women can learn to transfer their orgasm from self-stimulation to climaxing when they are together with their partner. But the outcome with coital orgasm varies. Actually when coital orgasm is not the universal goal outcome is excellent. With sex therapy those women whose physiologic orgastic threshold is sufficiently low to allow them to climax on coitus have a high probability of learning to do so. However, those couples wherein the woman's response pattern requires clitoral stimulation, learn to accept this and to have excellent mutually satisfying sex. To those who hold the belief that all women are capable of coital orgasm and that this is the only nonpathological pattern of sexual functioning the outcome of 25 to 50 percent of coital orgasm which can probably be achieved with sex therapy will be disappointing.[*]

Retarded ejaculation or the *orgastic dysfunctions of men* also have a mixed prognosis with sex therapy which varies directly with the severity of the condition. In its mild and partial forms, retarded ejaculation responds to sex therapy rapidly and almost universally. The more severe forms of this disorder seem to be inexorably linked with the patient's unconscious conflicts and resultant defenses, and severe forms of retarded ejaculation are often refractory to brief symptom-oriented forms of intervention.

The worst results with sex therapy unfortunately are with the totally *unresponsive woman*. Again, such a total suppression of sexual feelings is too often directly related to severe psychic damage and defenses against this to yield to brief intervention. The prognosis is better with secondary unresponsiveness, where it is often an expression of specific problems in the current relationship which can be resolved.

Intrapsychic Factors

It has been stated that superficial and surface anxieties such as performance anxiety often play a definitive role in the sexual dysfunctions. And this is true. Nevertheless, deeper kinds of psychic factors are also capable of producing sexual disturbances and often do.

In the analytic literature two basic unconscious conflicts which can produce sexual problems have been extensively considered and written about: unconscious fear of injury related to sexual behavior, and unconscious hostility toward the opposite gender. These are unquestionably important in producing sexual disturbances in some persons. When this is so, these issues must either be bypassed or resolved, at least to some degree, if the patient is to be able to function sexually.

[*] Again, evidence to support a definitive conclusion regarding the normalcy of coital orgasm is not yet available at this time.

175

Two other unconscious conflicts often contribute to sexual disorders. These have not been accorded as much attention and study as unconscious fear of injury and hostility. These are unconscious guilt about, and fear of, success and pleasure and the fear of intimacy and love.

Many persons in our culture are governed by an unconscious *self-destructive* pattern which makes pleasure and success somehow dangerous and forbidden. They are forever in conflict. On a conscious level they seek gratification. They strive for recognition, material success, beauty, pleasure in sex and love. But somehow, as they approach these normal and constructive human goals, they experience anxiety and/or guilt. These neurotic forces move them to sabotage their own efforts.

Such a self-destructive pleasure inhibition can act as a powerful obstacle to successful sex therapy. The outcome cannot be favorable in the face of such a dynamic if it is active. Guilt and anxiety about pleasure and success must be resolved or at least detoured in sex therapy before such a person can allow himself the intense pleasure of good sexual functioning. Of course, true resolution of this malignant conflict is the ultimate goal of therapy. When this can be accomplished, the patient's benefits extend considerably beyond his improved sexual functioning. However it is unfortunately not always possible to resolve pleasure conflicts, especially within the brief treatment format.

Sometimes when a patient is confronted with his pleasure inhibition in the course of sex therapy, he will then go on to seek reconstructive psychoanalytic therapy later on. Paradoxically if basic resolution is not feasible, it is sometimes possible to bypass this malignant and prevalent dynamic by fostering the patient's recognition of the fact that good sexual functioning is not equivalent to total happiness. Enjoyable sex is nice but will *not* really make him totally happy and successful. Sexual happiness is only a partial and limited kind of pleasure. He will still be able to suffer with his other inadequacies if he needs to. It goes without saying that this is a less than satisfactory outcome in terms of human values.

The fear of love, trust, and intimacy is also a malignant antitherapeutic force. Many persons are injured and disappointed early in life. Before they can deal with predatory attack on the basis of their own resources they must depend on parents and siblings to protect them. If this protection is less than perfect, and if the parents are hostile, destructive, or ambivalent—in other words if there are painful contingencies attached to this early intimacy—defenses are developed. These defenses often take the form of alienation and detachment. The child has to protect himself from pain by detaching and alienating himself and becoming prematurely emotionally independent. To ask such a defensively alienated, detached patient to touch, relate, and be intimate, which of course is done during the process of sex therapy, is like asking a jungle fighter to give up his knife. Reestablishment of the capacity to love and to trust and to move close to another person again is often a difficult process which takes time. During successful sex therapy this process is seldom complete, but often is given a good start as obstacles to its natural flow are gently removed.

The Relationship

Are human beings basically a bonding species? What is the relationship between bonding and sex? We do not yet have the answers to such fundamental questions, and yet they are crucial to our complete understanding of human sexuality. Clearly there are complex correlations between human sexual functioning and the quality of the relationship between the partners. Indeed the nature of the relationship is an important prognostic factor in predicting the outcome of sex therapy.

Many subhuman species form a mating bond with a member of the opposite sex and have sexual intercourse only with that individual. In some species these bonds last only during the mating and/or breeding season, in others the exclusive sexual bond is for life. On the other hand other species including our nearest primate relatives do not form such bonds at all. Males mate with any female in heat.

Clinical evidence suggests that human beings are probably a bonding species, although it is not clear whether we are lifetime bonders or time-limited courtship bonders. Falling in love, the human correlate of bonding, is a highly predictable behavioral pattern which begins when the brain is flooded with sex hormones during adolescence. Most persons feel better and more secure when they are engaged in a love

177

relationship. They enjoy sex with the person they love more than with a stranger with whom there is no emotional connection. However, some persons do not fall in love or their love and sexual relationships may show distorted patterns. Thus some men and women function best sexually with a variety of partners or with partners with whom they have limited relationships or who are emotionally unavailable. Most authorities believe that nonbonding or promiscuous sexual patterns represent a pathological inhibition of the natural human tendency to form love relationships, but definitive evidence on this matter is lacking.

Whatever our "natural" biologically programmed behavioral tendency may ultimately be found to be, it is only *one* of many determinants which govern our dyadic and sexual behavior. Learned or experiential components are, of course, of inestimable weight in determining of final love and sex responses.

Given our incomplete knowledge on this subject, clinical observation suggests that the healthy guilt-free person is not dependent on being in love for his sexual functioning and pleasure. He *can* function well sexually and experience erotic pleasure and lust in the absence of an intense affectionate or romantic relationship, as long as the relationship is neither destructive nor the sex object repugnant. However, a feeling of love between the partners makes sex an infinitely more satisfying, pleasurable, and human experience. Love is the only real aphrodisiac.

While love is not absolutely necessary, hostility and rejection and fear of the partner can be very destructive to sexual functioning. Indeed when an essentially hostile relationship exists between the partners who are seeking help for a sexual dysfunction, the prognosis is guarded. It is irrational to attempt sex therapy unless a reasonably affectionate relationship exists between the couple. It is difficult and perhaps not even desirable to attempt to foster a sexual relationship when such deep rejection of the partner exists that the idea of giving him or allowing him to give her pleasure evokes intense anger or fear. Such emotion may outright prevent cooperation in the treatment process. More subtly, if anger or fear is unconscious, there may be overt cooperation but, predictably, the angry or rejecting partner will covertly sabotage sex therapy.

However, it is possible to get couples to function sexually if they are

178

The kiss

not in love, if some affection exists even though they are relatively detached, just as long as they are not basically hostile to each other. This
happens when surrogates are employed in sex therapy. However, while
getting two "strangers" to function sexually with one another, whether
they are married or whether they are paid surrogates, may have some
merit, it is hardly emotionally satisfying for the patients or for most
therapists.

The best prognosis in sex therapy exists when there is a real bond of
love between the couple. If they truly love, if they are truly connected,
if they truly feel for one another, then anything is possible. Even the
most tenacious dysfunction is likely to yield when a real love bond
exists.

Sex therapy cannot create love. However, in its process it frequently
can remove obstacles to the experience and expression of love. And
when such obstacles and defenses to love exist, their removal is the first
order of business for the sex therapist.